Acclaim for *Shakespeare's Rev.........*

H. Ronald Hulnick, Ph.D., President, University of Santa Monica, Co-author with Mary R. Hulnick, Ph.D., of *Loyalty to Your Soul: The Heart of Spiritual Psychology* 'This is a brilliant gem of metaphorical, Spiritual connections between William Shakespeare and Spiritual Psychology. In thoroughly exploring Shakespeare's plays with wisdom, clarity, and wit, Paul Hunting masterfully demonstrates how the very human experiences in Shakespeare's plays are indeed 'devoted to one thing – to remind us of our true spiritual nature as a loving soul.' Hunting's insights and exegesis of Shakespeare, the Bible, and Spiritual Psychology principles can only serve to speed the world's Spiritual Awakening, as individuals find answers to two essential questions – 'Who am I?' and 'What is my purpose?' – in the reading of this fascinating book.'

Paul Kaye, D.S.S. 'Absolutely fascinating.'

Marjorie Salinas 'Finally, Will makes sense! Thanks.'

Catherine Corona Ph.D. 'This is amazing, Paul.'

Courtney Pierce 'This is absolutely gorgeous. Thank you for undertaking such a task, Paul. Wow. I'm in awe and inspired!'

Cirelle Raphalian 'So interesting! Thanks for parting the curtain.'

Stephen McGhee 'What you wrote about is amazing! You are a true leader.'

Elisa Novick 'Stunning!'

Janis Fitzgerald 'Soft stillness and the night become the touches of sweet harmony ... Let's sit here and let the music fill our ears ... even the smallest star sings like an angel in its motion ... draw her home with music. Yes Paul – well done! Well done indeed!'

Ann Webre 'What an interesting idea! '

Amy Bransky 'Light, loving, and honouring to your tribute and expression.'

Heather Brown 'Beautiful.'

Coco Rose 'I love it!!!'

Barbara Wieland 'Paul. You have a marvellous way with words.'

Revelation

[Rev-uh-ley-shuhn]

something revealed or disclosed,

especially a striking disclosure, as of

something not before realised.

'What follows…underlines our premise: if you don't understand *The Tempest*, you don't understand Shakespeare – and if you don't understand Shakespeare, you don't understand yourself.'

– From the book, pg 202.

Shakespeare's Revelation

His Hidden Key to Spiritual Fulfilment

PAUL HUNTING

TrueSelf Publishing

ISBN: 978-0-9955370-0-2
eISBN (ePub): 978-0-9955370-2-6
eISBN (Kindle): 978-0-9955370-1-9

Typeset by Mach 3 Solutions Ltd (www.mach3solutions.co.uk)
Printed by Lightning Source

Published by:
TrueSelf Publishing
Thornfield
Stretton on Fosse
Moreton-in-Marsh
GL56 9RA
UK

DEDICATION

I dedicate this book, and all that flows from it, to my teacher and great example,
John-Roger; and to the amazing human being, John Morton,
who has so gracefully taken up the staff
of that ancient line of Spiritual Warriors.

ACKNOWLEDGMENTS

Most of us have an inner critic who does his best to undermine us – especially if we go out on a limb like I have with this book. Without the constant, unfailing support, encouragement, cooling breezes of clear-thinking, and some damn good ideas from Geri, my lovely wife, I'd have keeled over with self-doubt a year ago.

If Dr Lin Morel, my soul-centred coach, had not been so absolutely certain my next step was to write the book of my life, this would still be as forgotten as my original title: *The Forgotten Self*.

To acknowledge fully my network of wonderful friends, who have contributed in ways they probably don't even realise, would make a chapter in itself. The synopsis of such a chapter is to give very special thanks to Anja Leigh-Russell, Catherine Corona, Cindy Lou Golin, Martyn Stanbridge, David Sand, Leigh Taylor-Young Morton, Dominic Mafham, Anton Lesser, Sam Westmacott, Sarah Dawkins, Peter Dawkins and Saira Salmon.

And good old-fashioned plain ordinary thanks to all my friends on FaceBook and in my local village of Stretton on Fosse, Stratford-upon-Avon, Warwickshire, England, who allowed themselves to be guinea pigs for my first presentation of these ideas. Also those in the Village Caff in Blockley who put up with my spending hours there over one Americano lost in the trance of writing.

To all who helped make this book a reality, I offer a huge 'Thank You'.

CONTENTS

DEDICATION   v

ACKNOWLEDGEMENTS   vi

AUTHOR'S FOREWORD   ix

INTRODUCTION   I

   Shakespeare's Paradigm   2

   Invisible Ink   18

PART I   SHAKESPEARE'S GENESIS   37

   Chapter One, *Richard II*   42

     The Deposing of the Soul

   Chapter Two, *Othello*   62

     Satan's Plot

   Chapter Three, *Macbeth*   86

     The Loss and Restoration of the Holy Grail

PART 2   SHAKESPEARE'S GOSPEL   121

   Chapter Four, *The Merchant of Venice*   121

     The Word Made Flesh

   Chapter Five, *Henry V*   140

     The Resurrection and Ascension of the Soul

PART 3   SHAKESPEARE'S REVELATION   171

    Chapter Six, *Hamlet*   171

      The Dilemma of Man

    Chapter Seven, *The Tempest*   202

      Shakespeare's Revelation — Unconditional Forgiveness at the End of Time

EPILOGUE   230

REFERENCES   234

THE FORGOTTEN SELF

'Thus conscience doth make cowards of us all. And thus the native hue of resolution is sicklied o'er with the pale caste of thought. And enterprises of great pith and moment, with this regard, their currents turn awry, and lose the name of action.' – Hamlet, Act 3, Scene I.

Knowing Who You Really Are

If I've learned anything from 35 years as a soul-centred coach, it's that unless you are in touch with your true self it is virtually impossible to lead a truly fulfilling life.

The pandemic of a false sense of identity has millions of us chasing meaningless goals that, at best, bring a fleeting satisfaction. A life spent over-compensating for persistent feelings of frustration, unworthiness, fear, guilt, resentment, and disappointment might be 'normal' – but it's far from necessary.

Knowing who you really are, having a true sense of purpose, and centring your life in authentic values, goals and actions is essential to a life filled with healthy, deeply rewarding relationships, true wealth, abundance, an abiding sense of inner confidence and security – and even sustainable levels of joy and ecstasy (without the need for artificial stimulants).

We all know Shakespeare was a genius and an imparter of great truth and wisdom. What few people have realised is he was also a master spiritual teacher who has hidden in his works the ancient spiritual keys to an abundantly fulfilling life as well as absolute spiritual liberation.

A Word about Words

To paraphrase one of Shakespeare's many momentous lines, 'that which we call a soul would by any other word smell as sweet', I'm going to be using words like God, Satan, Adam, Eve, Cain, Abel, Serpent, day, night, darkness, light, etc. – a lot. The main reason being – so does Shakespeare! This in no way means I personally believe they exist or existed as real beings. On the contrary. My conviction is they are metaphorical personifications of core states of consciousness that function within all human beings. I am delineating them with these terminologies because in our (Judeo-Christian) culture they are used extensively in the Bible, Torah, literature, and common parlance. That's just what we tend to call them. If your culture, religion, or belief system uses different words for the same states of consciousness, then I sincerely invite you to substitute whatever words you would use. In other words, please don't let the word-levels block you from the value of receiving Shakespeare's most generous gift to us.

The Conversation

This book is the beginning of a new conversation – not just about Shakespeare, the Bible and religion, but about who we really are as human beings and what on earth we're doing here on earth. When you reach 'the end' you'll see I am simply pausing, taking a breath, and waiting for a response.

Your response.

This entire book is the opening sentence in a massive new conversation. A conversation that I sincerely invite you to make as much yours as mine.

You can make contact, ask questions, share your insights and revelations at any time through my website at www.ShakespearesRevelation.com

For many of us this conversation is going to develop a new paradigm bringing a greater depth of exploration about who we really are as human beings, and why we're here going round and round in space held in perfect balance on the surface of this planet by a mysterious force called gravity.

Shakespeare is continuously pointing out that the majority of us have falsely defined 'who we are' in terms of powerful beliefs, ancient traditions, and turbulent feelings that often have very little to do with the Truth.

Although his plays can be experienced on many dimensions, in this book, I'm focussing on three in particular:

- 1   Physical story

- 2   Psycho-spiritual allegory

- 3   Mystical–theological discourse

It is through combining these levels with his sublime genius, Shakespeare has not only brought joy into our hearts, he's also given us the profound key to a true understanding of who we really are and how to fulfil our spiritual destiny. This is a hidden key that when found unlocks Truths unrecognised in the scriptures for thousands of years. A key he has hidden in a labyrinth of gloriously cryptic, twisting, turning ways in his plots, themes and poetic imagery. I've done my best to unravel what I can – but I refuse to over-simplify his richness into something banal. Consequently, this depth and quality of conversation will not interest everyone.

Why so deeply hidden (as are the mystical allusions unseen in the above quote from Hamlet's 'to be or not to be' soliloquy)? Maybe because in his day, humanity wasn't yet ready to hear the greater Truth. Maybe because the Church and Crown would have been less than open and receptive to a Truth that clarifies centuries of theological misunderstanding and puts true freedom of choice into each and everyone's own hands.

Maybe because to receive Shakespeare's inner spiritual gift we need to stretch our minds and open our hearts a lot more than is comfortable.

I do hope you enjoy reading *Shakespeare's Revelation* as much as I enjoyed writing it.

If you don't – tell no one.

If you do – tell everyone!

Paul Hunting, May 2016

INTRODUCTION

'You are here to enable the divine purpose of the universe to unfold. That is how important you are.' – Eckhart Tolle.

B efore we begin this journey, perhaps you'd like to take a journal and, as best you can right now, answer these two fundamental questions:

- Who are you – really?

- Why are you here?

As Shakespeare's submerged Truths bubble to the surface, allow the spiritual wisdom that is the Truth in you to awaken. He speaks of ancient concepts and spiritual practice that have been unrecognised even by many of today's most aware and enlightened teachers. It would seem even enlightenment itself has no end.

Treat yourself to a beautiful new journal. Write reflections, insights, dreams and questions. What issues are troubling you in your life? What outcomes would you rather see?

Along the way I shall prompt you. When you get to the end I'll ask again. Who are you, why are you here? See how your sense of purpose has clarified for you. How does it feel to be more sure of yourself and your destiny? Don't be concerned about confusion along the way. The universe itself was born of chaos. Confusion is a sign of an inner stirring. Being stirred is good. So is being shaken. So be gentle with yourself as you explore the undiscovered country.

Shakespeare's Paradigm

The next exercise is to begin seeing Shakespeare himself through a different lens. Think of him as a different being from simply *'the bard'* or *'the actor from Stratford.'* Elevate him to the level of Jesus Christ, Mohammed, Buddha, Krishna, Shiva, Plato, Aristotle ... see him as a great master and enlightened spiritual teacher ... and then listen to what his works say to you.

Cryptic Clues

Although they make compelling drama, I am personally sceptical about the idea of secret codes and conspiracy theories lying at the heart of sacred writings and scripture. But there it is. This book uncovers the same codes and hidden meanings contained not only throughout Shakespeare's canon, but the Bible as well. It's as if Shakespeare's mission was to recreate the misunderstood key biblical Truths into new and more accessible forms as an antidote to the way the scriptures have been corrupted into the weapons of mass destruction they were never intended to be.

Unlock your Soul

I am not a spiritual teacher. I do not presume to be anyone's guide. I am, however, an experienced coach. I have been working with a *'soul-centred paradigm'* for more than 35 years. What I will do is make some suggestions for you to reflect on based on my own personal journey of discovery and questions my clients have found useful over the last three decades.

It goes without saying (as they say) – please feel free to adopt, adapt, improve on or totally ignore any or all of my suggestions.

Shakespeare's Globe

'But pardon, and gentles all, the flat unraised spirits that have dared on this unworthy scaffold to bring forth so great an object.' – Chorus, *Henry V.*

The very stage upon which so many of Shakespeare's characterisations and allegories drew their first breath was itself used as a great metaphor of our life in general, *'All the world's a stage, and all the men and women merely players; they have their exits and their entrances, and one man in his time plays many parts, his acts being seven ages.'* (*As You Like It*, Act 2, Scene 7). And, concealed within his metaphors, allusions, and word-play, is where his deeper secrets and keys lie hidden waiting patiently for us to be ready to find them.

While new paradigms are usually rejected by the mainstream (and rightly so – the cutting-edge must be tempered in the fires of doubt), there are notable exceptions. There are some highly-respected citizens of The World of Shakespeare who recognise, seek, and encourage the quest for greater understanding of themselves and ways Shakespeare's hidden gems can help us all find spiritual succour.

'I share Peter's belief that Shakespeare's work was intended by the author to help us create a garden for our souls.' – Mark Rylance, Artistic Director of the Globe Theatre, in his Foreword to *The Wisdom of Shakespeare in The Tempest* by Peter Dawkins.

Having now abandoned all reason – along with the original manuscript I was working on – I have spent the last year in a frenzy of writing, personal insights, and revelations.

To make sense of the confetti on my laptop and in my brain, I tried articulating all manner of paradigm shifts to see what might help.

Eventually a helpful one emerged already endorsed by another writer as equally fascinated by hidden mystical teachings:

'The teachings of the Bible pervade and underlie all his plays to such a degree that the plays seem, in fact, to be dramatised commentaries on and examples of the scriptural teachings.' – Peter Dawkins, *The Wisdom of Shakespeare in The Tempest.*

Rather than look at the canon as 37 individual plays, what if it were like a brilliant diamond with 37 facets all reflecting different aspects of the same story? The story of who we really are, how we were deposed by a tyrant and how we can reclaim our forgotten self? A biblical allegory told from multiple viewing points all very different from orthodox church doctrine?

Madness.

How could there be any sane connection between say, *Richard II, Othello* and *Macbeth*? Or *Henry V* and *The Merchant of Venice*? Or *Hamlet* and *The Tempest*? Or all of these and *King Lear*?

Madness.

But there is. There really is. From the level of 'play-and-character' you cannot see it. From a higher, more holistic perspective, you can gestalt the invisible metaphor Shakespeare uses all the time.

What if all the characters populating the *outer* worlds he creates are metaphors for the different states of consciousness populating our *inner* world.

What if there's a singular thread running through the entire canon that transforms even Shakespeare's incomparable genius into an even greater cornucopia of ancient spiritual secrets? A thread that leads to true spiritual fulfilment for all who have the eyes to see and the ears to hear?

He seems to do this in two ways:

❧ By not using characters as such, but by 'shape-shifting' just three pairs of core archetypes that appear consistently in every play.

❧ By continuously alluding to in his verse and dramatising in his plotting, the ancient secret of the Sound Current. This is known throughout the world's scriptures as The Word, the waters, the wind from heaven, the wind invisible, and many other terms. For over thirty years I've been studying in depth the teachings of the Sound Current – this is how I was so able to recognise Shakespeare's myriad subliminal references. What I have begun to do is bring them to the surface – because to have dedicated his entire works to expressing this fundamental Truth, he must have considered it vitally important.

Of course, this needs more than a little explaining.

So far, my attempts at sharing my new discoveries with the World of Shakespeare have felt like informing the Pope about a new contraceptive. But if you're one of the many millions who crave the light behind the shadows in Christian theology or seek authentic, dogma-free, straight-from-the-heart-of-God spiritual guidance in our increasingly secular modern society – stick around.

Disappointed you will not be. If you do happen to be a 'Shakespeare Fan' with a mind open long enough to reach the last few pages – the final revelation is guaranteed to make your jaw hit the floor.

Humanity's Biggest Problems: Our Biggest Opportunity for True Spiritual Fulfilment

As a soul-centred coach, the biggest problem I see facing each of us and all humanity, a problem threatening our very survival on this planet, is not climate change, peak oil, pollution, population explosion, or even the unstoppable virus of fanatical terrorism.

5

Our biggest problem is the true *cause* of all these ills. Ills that have forged a world where it seems that however much we right wrongs and fight evils, it seems impossible for us to live together in peace and enjoy the earth's bounty.

A cause that drives us to compensate in self-destructive ways for an itch we can never scratch, a hunger we can never satisfy, and an ache that never goes away no matter how much we numb it out.

Unlikely as it may seem, this true cause is best expressed as: *we have forgotten who we really are and why we're here.*

What if we are all souls who have forgotten we are divine? Forgotten the *Ananda* we once knew? And we believe whatever the mind says we are — often based on the assertions of others whose opinion we value more than our own? Do you really believe we're a random bag of chemicals that was created by a freak accident of physics? Many do.

Humanity suffers from Spiritual Amnesia on a global scale.

When we lose our true sense of spiritual guidance and connection that's exactly how we feel — lost!

And it's that 'lost' feeling of what the existentialist Sartre calls '*Anguish, abandonment, and despair*' that drives us to all manner of destructive, meaningless measures.

It seems Shakespeare's plays are devoted to one thing — to remind us of our true spiritual nature as a loving soul, the divine Sound (son) of God. He also spares no blood in warning us of the futility and consequences of pursuing a life worshiping the false gods of 'good and evil'.

The toughest concept for us in the West to get our heads around is what exactly it is we lost; and how on earth we can claim it back. I'm just going to tell it straight from the hip – we've got a few hundred pages left for this tricky concept to find a home in that place where you keep your precious gems of information.

Here goes: Shakespeare's symbolism for that which humanity lost is *the tempest.*

Biblically, throughout time what he calls 'tempests' throughout his plays has also been referred to as: the Sound Current, the Word, the waters, and the wind from heaven ... among many other symbols, metaphors and poetic allusions. It seems it is this sacred sound of God's Name that was sealed off in the beginning when the first soul was beguiled by the fatal attractions of this world.

Once you 'get' this, everything else falls into place.

All You Have to do to 'Get it'

At university, I specialised in two areas: symbolic logic and psycholinguistics. My research shows all we have to do to see what's hidden in Shakespeare's verse is to undertake a '*complex cognitive process of decoding symbols in order to construct or derive meaning*'.

In other words, keep doing what you're doing right now – reading.

The skill required to receive Shakespeare's revelation is – reading. Defined by linguists as '*a complex cognitive process of decoding symbols in order to construct or derive meaning*'.

I'll do my best to bring the deep structure of his language to the surface. All you have to do is read it – and maybe open your heart to a new way of seeing.

Paradigm Shift: A New Way of Seeing

Jesuit Pierre Teilhard de Chardin, to the chagrin of the church, notoriously asserted, '*We are not human beings having a spiritual experience. We are spiritual beings having a human experience*'.

This is one of the basic tenets of spiritual psychology. Reframing our experiences through soul-centred eyes facilitates an instantaneous paradigm shift and healing transformation.

Our paradigms, sometimes called 'comfort zones' are the nexus of beliefs, attitudes, values, and philosophies with which we (try to) keep a sense of balance, security and meaning. This is how we make sense of all the inner conflict, mystery, uncertainty, enigma, paradox and fear that life throws at us. While they may give us a fragile feeling of understanding and confidence, there is absolutely no correlation whatsoever between our belief system and the Truth. While it may keep us feeling safe, it is always under threat of exposure, it always keeps us ensnared. Unless we're willing to risk letting go of our old paradigm we will never expand into the Truth of who we really are, we must always settle for one meagre bowl of porridge.

Psychologists and philosophers have generated dozens of 'paradigm shift' images. They all demonstrate how the same visual information gives rise to different internal perceptions and experiences depending on your point of view.

Wittgenstein's rabbit–duck will serve here. Or is it a rabbit–seagull?

My point is we don't lose the rabbit if we see the seagull, we gain a seagull – and a duck. We don't lose our ground-level perspective if we fly up to the clouds and look down. The ground-level is still there. However our biggest obstacle to all good things, from clear communication with loved ones to complete spiritual fulfilment, is our resistance to new ideas, information, and experiences. Anything truly new that could add value to our knowledge-base is so often felt as a threat that has to be beaten off with a stick. We hang on to our beliefs and mind-centred paradigms as if our life depends on them. Unfortunately, the reality often is – our life depends on letting them go.

If this applies to you, then the rest of this book is going to be tough. Because from now on we're going to be looking at ourselves and Shakespeare's plays from a soul-centred paradigm. And the key to letting go of old beliefs is to focus not on our point of view (because we compulsively defend this) but on the viewing point.

The viewing point is that of the soul.

In an interview about his role as Othello at the National Theatre, David Harewood said, *'Love him or hate him, if you don't understand Othello, I don't think you understand yourself.'*

I totally agree and I'd go even further, *'If you don't understand Shakespeare, I don't think you understand yourself.'*

And we can't understand Shakespeare until we see his writings through the soul-centred paradigm I am convinced he, too, looks through.

Shakespeare's Soul-Centred Paradigm

'That's one small step for a man, one giant leap for mankind.' – Neil Armstrong, moon landing, 1969.

Armstrong's iconic moon walk symbolises what you can do right now. If you're willing to risk that one small step of letting go your resistance to new perspectives and begin to see through your soul's eyes you also take a giant leap into a more authentic and fulfilling life.

I do not think our existential challenge is to change all the things we don't like about this world so we can be more comfortable. And I don't think we need to 'change ourselves' either. From the soul's viewing point, we're absolutely perfect right now. The greatest act of power we humans have is not a nuclear bomb – it's our ability to shift paradigms, to see the seagulls in the rabbits, to see the abiding spiritual Truth in Shakespeare's soul.

If we truly want a sustainable future for ourselves and our children ... if we truly want fresh air we can breathe, food that cleanses and nourishes us, an end to starvation, tyranny, and exploitation, as unlikely as it may sound, we need to raise our viewing point to tap into the infinite source of wisdom, power, creativity, and love that resides right now deep inside us.

Shakespeare makes literally thousands of, what appear to be, kosher biblical references and allusions. But they're not. Even today the mediaeval interpretations of the ancient scriptures are as fiercely defended by cries of 'sin!', 'heresy!', and 'blasphemy!' as they are dismissed by cries of 'nonsense!', 'unscientific!' and 'superstitious!'. No wonder new insight into our nature and purpose here is kept under ground. But if we dig beneath the surface of Shakespeare's sacred writings, and assume the soul's viewing point, we can see how with invisible ink, he is truly offering us a way out of the dilemmas and the agony of being a spiritual being trapped in a mortal form with no viable exit strategy.

From 'Overthought' to 'Underthought'

'Gerard Manley Hopkins draws a distinction between the poet's 'overthought' or explicit meaning, and his 'underthought' or the meaning given by the progression of images and metaphors. But it is the 'underthought' that is the real poetic meaning, and the explicit meaning must conform to it.' — Northrop Frye, on Canada.

Armed with our secret weapon, the sword of truth, let us blast off together into the undiscovered country of Shakespeare's 'underthought'. Here's the itinerary. See if you can spot the pattern emerging:

- The three selves of soul-centred psychology

- The three selves of Shakespeare's Genesis

- The three selves of Portia's caskets

- The three selves of Lear's portions

The Three Selves of Soul-Centred Psychology

'*Ontogeny recapitulates phylogeny.*' – Ernst Haeckel, 19th Century biologist and philosopher.

The phrase 'ontogeny recapitulates phylogeny' is shorthand for saying our development in the womb traces the same steps as our development as a species.

One of the reasons I believe I was so able to read Shakespeare's invisible ink is that the 'three-selves', soul-centred coaching model I, and others in this field, have been using for more than thirty years follows the same pattern seen in all his plays.

The really interesting thing about this model is that it's not just a theory. It's empirically verifiable. I have been using it with unparalleled success with many hundreds of clients.

Over twenty years back, I began to discover a way of working with the basic instincts of horses to enable clients to have an experience of the power of authenticity. Clients don't usually come to me asking for 'spiritual awakening' but for a breakthrough in their leadership. I very rarely use the 'S' words in our sessions – unless they bring them up. Because leadership is simply another word for relationship I ask them about relationships where they might feel intimidated, unable to communicate effectively or influence positively. As you can imagine, even senior leaders have no shortage of material.

Before I sketch out my 'three circles', I tell them I work with horses because they only follow us if we're being authentic, true to ourselves. It's phenomenal. They really won't. They seem uncannily capable of reading our energy and sensing our intention. If our intention is not clear, meaning we're unconsciously pretending something about ourselves, they treat us like a predator. They run away. Switch off. Or defend themselves if we become violent. It's rare, honest, instantaneous feedback. The converse is also true. If we find that place of authenticity inside us, they will give us their heart. It's deeply moving. It blows me away every time – even after twenty years on the trot.

In the centre of the three circles is 'who I really am'. This is the original self, the state of pure goodness and innocence we are born with.

THE 3 SELVES OF
SPIRITUAL PSYCHOLOGY

"Ontogeny recapitulates phylogeny"

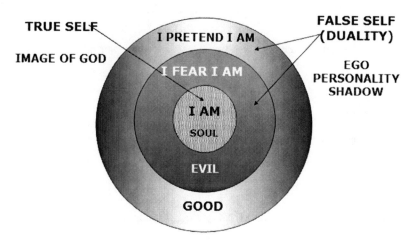

As we develop, we unconsciously try to form a sense of identity. We are hard-wired, it seems, to define ourselves in terms of our feelings. If we *feel* bad, we decide we *are* bad. Intuitively we know this to be a lie, but if we are told 'no', 'don't', 'stop' a hundred times a day and constantly made to feel bad, naughty, stupid, lazy, etc., this fundamental lie becomes a compelling Truth that can drive the entire course of our life. These feelings of unworthiness become a major part of our self-concept – the inner circle: 'I'm afraid I am an evil person'.

13

To assuage the fear, guilt and pain of this erroneous self-concept, we find creative ways to prove we're not who we are afraid we are. We create a self-image to project into the world in order to protect ourselves from hurt, and get approval from others. We also look in the mirror at our image to kill the pain and convince ourselves we are ok. Our self-image, the outer circle, becomes: 'I pretend I am a good person.'

Bottom line, instead of living through one true self, we have three selves vying for the central position in our consciousness: the true self plus twin false selves. Who I really am is a pure, innocent, absolutely perfect soul. But this Truth is overshadowed by the two lies: I am afraid I am 'evil'. I pretend I am 'not-evil'.

The Three Selves of Shakespeare's Genesis

'Two such opposed Kings encamp them still in man as well as herbs, grace and rude will: And where the worser is predominant, full soon the canker death eats up that plant.' — Friar Laurence, *Romeo and Juliet*, Act 2, Scene 3.

Looking at Genesis from a soul-centre, we can see it as the metaphorical account of how the energies known as Satan became the god of our false selves. How he usurped the soul as 'king' of our inner world, caused us to forget who we really are. Made us believe he was God. This is the hidden theology behind all Shakespeare's plays.

The expression *'ontogeny recapitulates phylogeny'* was originally coined by Ernst Haeckel to describe our biological development as an embryo. It works just as well with our spiritual evolution. In Part One, we'll look in fascinating detail at how Shakespeare reveals his paradigm of Genesis. For now I want to point out how much sense Genesis actually makes when we read it — not as a myth of the creation of the physical world — but as a metaphor of the creation of the human consciousness.

No more do we need to cast the baby Genesis out with the bathwater. No more do we need to stretch our mental acrobatics to their limit bridging the gap between seven days and thirteen billion years. No longer do science and scripture remain mutually exclusive.

Unsullied by dogma, the scripture is actually clear, relevant and helpful to a contemporary understanding of who we are and how humanity came to be in such dire straits: Adam and Eve were not the first couple on earth to live in sin. Putting these two passages together, it is obvious they are not 'persons' at all, but an archetype of the male–female polarity of the original emanation from God, the soul.

'*So God created man in his own image, in the image of God created he him; male and female created he them.*' – Genesis 1:27.

'*And the Lord God formed man of the dust of the ground, and breathed into his nostrils the breath of life; and man became a living soul.*' – Genesis 2:7.

The image of God is 'male and female'. Eve was a side of Adam (Adam's rib). Adam and Eve was a single soul. There it is!

Later, while in the blissful state of consciousness we call paradise, heaven, or Ananda, as far as we can express the inexpressible in words, the soul was lured into absorbing a base level of consciousness called 'Good and Evil'. The opposite polarities of Good and Evil are now represented by the paired archetypes Cain and Abel. Not only did 'Good and Evil' usurp the soul as ruler of its kingdom, but Cain murdered his brother Abel, became cursed with eternal perdition, and planted the karmic seeds of the eternal bitterness and unremitting hatred between our own inner levels, brother nations, creeds, and all manner of enterprises we see every day on the Ten O'clock News.

Within us we now have three selves. The true self, the soul, neutrally observing, unconditionally loving and forgiving. And the twin warring brothers 'Good and Evil' characterised in Genesis as 'Cain and Abel'. Cain and Abel make so much noise and cause so much pain we become totally distracted from the sweet sound of the soul that serenades us from within.

ADAM AND EVE

"*And the serpent said unto the woman, Ye shall not surely die: For God doth know that in the day ye eat thereof, then your eyes shall be opened, and ye shall be as gods, knowing good and evil.*"

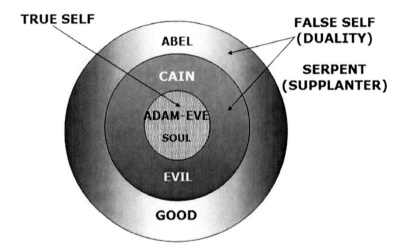

In this light, our empirical ontogeny is an exact replica of our biblical phylogeny. This is how the spiritual–psycho-genetics was laid down in the beginning of time as our three selves (three states of consciousness).

Who I really am is the soul. Who I am afraid I am is evil. Who I pretend to be is good. Good and evil may well be opposed, but no more so than heads and tails are on opposite sides of the coin. The one needs the other to exist as much as the duck needs the rabbit. The inconvenient Truth is that good and evil are made from the same metal, cast from the same die. This is why the fight against evil is always futile, always a losing battle no matter which side seems to win.

The greater Truth is that neither good nor evil exists. They are both shadows caused by the light of the world, the soul. The light eclipsed by the serpent in the beginning. What we believe and base our lives on is the non-existent shadow of the hidden reality Shakespeare is quickening inside us every time we see a play.

Guess from whom this apocryphal quote comes:

'Evil does not exist, or at least not unto itself. Evil is simply the relative absence of God. It is, just like darkness and cold, a word human beings created to describe the absence of God. God did not create evil. What we call evil is the result of what happens when a person is unaware of the presence of God's love in our heart. It's like the cold that comes when there is no heat or the darkness that comes when there is no light.' – Albert Einstein (from *Loyalty to your Soul,* Drs Ron and Mary Hulnick).

As Shakespeare spares no ink in pointing out, the fallacy of most religions is that we are inherently evil (sinners) and to be saved we must become good. Shakespeare says, we are already perfect in God's eyes, what we need to do so we can step into the awareness of this is forgive ourselves unconditionally – and listen to the sounds of the wind.

As you'll soon see, the allegory of 'the pretender killing his brother (sometimes metaphorically) and usurping his throne' is told and retold by Shakespeare throughout – including, most notably in *Richard II, Othello, Macbeth, Hamlet,* and *The Tempest.*

In *East of Eden,* in similar vein to Shakespeare, John Steinbeck takes one Hebrew word from Genesis, 'timshel', reinterprets it from 'thou shalt' to 'thou mayest' and crafts his famous fable of Adam, Eve, Serpent, Cain, and Abel. He, however, comes to the cynical conclusion:

'I believe that there is one story in the world, and only one ... Humans are caught – in their lives, in their thoughts, in their hungers and ambitions, in their avarice and cruelty, and in their kindness and

17

generosity too — in a net of good and evil ... There is no other story. A man, after he has brushed off the dust and chips of his life, will have left only the hard, clean questions: Was it good or was it evil? Have I done well — or ill?'

Many would no doubt agree. He voices the perception of most philosophy and religion. I agree that at the level of 'good and evil' life has no meaning. But surely we're here as a soul to gain experience of God's creation. Any experience. All experiences are just that — experiences. Hitler's experience was just as valid AS AN EXPERIENCE as Mother Theresa's. From the mind-centre this is an appalling thing for us to even think. But from a soul-centre we simply do not know! The mind has to judge. It has to be right. The soul simply observes and loves everyone and everything.

Based on the level of consciousness expressed in his works, Shakespeare sees the transcendent Truth in Genesis, Gospels, and Revelation that trumps everything sense, mind and reason tells us is so.

The Invisible Ink

We're now going to apply some heat to the invisible ink through which Shakespeare whispers his deeper story. These are the keys to his secret language, hidden for 400 years.

The Three Selves of Portia's Caskets

The question here is: what is the quirky little charade we will now explore really about? Is it just folderol? Or is it the key to Shakespeare's intention — to wake us up to the Truth of who we really are, what happened to make us forget this, and how we can awaken from the midsummer night's dream we believe is reality?

18

All I've done here is look for the 'underthought'. It clarifies once we set an intention. It's like crosswords, they get easier once you get to know the mind-set of the compiler. Getting to know Shakespeare's mind-set and cryptic language is an infinitely worthwhile endeavour.

The Merchant of Venice has always been my favourite play. Maybe because my mother loved it so well. A petite Jewess with a wry sense of humour, she would often relate the time she played Shylock in her school play (this I would love to have seen). I was five when I first heard about '*three thousand ducats for three months*'. Why would anyone want so many duck eggs for so long?

This edgy, gripping, easily misunderstood, underrated play weaves multiple profound spiritual allegories together camouflaged against a back-cloth of stunning mystical significance. More will be revealed in Part 2: Shakespeare's Gospel. For now, I want to tease out the strand that tells us how he pits his entire cast of characters against each other to tell his one hidden story.

The film version, starring Al Pacino as Shylock and Jeremy Irons as Antonio, is the most sumptuous production in my personal cache of DVD's. Yet it is the wise, beautiful, infinitely wealthy Portia (Lynn Collins) who steps in to serve our purpose here.

[Stop reading here. Watch this quintessential film now. And resume.]

The Merchant of Venice is a fulcrum upon which all the other ingredients of Shakespeare's theology balance.

Of all his plays, the metaphor of Portia's three caskets offers the clearest exposition of the 3-Selves model of human consciousness Shakespeare uses to drive archetypes, plots, allegories and characterisations throughout. *The Merchant of Venice* is truly a masterclass in how to plant the gene of peace into our DNA and undermine a tyranny that dictates *from the moment we are born,* what we believe, how we think and how we should behave.

At the Rabbit-level of story, it is a gripping play dancing on the edge of anti-Semitism and the revenge of the spat upon. It holds up a mirror to us all when we feel justified in sneering at those we do not understand. Slightly deeper, it tells of the love between two men, where Antonio seems to be willing to lay down his life for his beloved friend Bassanio.

There are several sub-plots but the main through line is as follows: To enable Bassanio to court the beautiful, wealthy, Portia, the woman with whom he is destined to know true love, he asks Antonio to lend him three thousand ducats. With all his money invested in his cargos at sea, Antonio feels he is left no choice but to borrow the money from Shylock. Shylock is a Jew and a usurer. The mutual hatred between Shylock and Antonio more than balances the mutual love between Bassanio and Antonio. Shylock agrees to lend Antonio three thousand ducats for three months on the condition that if he defaults, Shylock is entitled by legally binding bond to carve a pound of flesh from Antonio's breast. To pay off his debt, Antonio gives his word away to Shylock. He gambles on the safe return of his ships and cargo well before the cut-off date. In so doing he casts his fate to the 'tempest', in Shylock's foreshadowing words, *'the peril of waters, winds, and rocks.'* — *The Merchant of Venice,* Act I, Scene 3.

While Antonio waits for his ships to come home, Bassanio uses the cash to win the hand of the divine Portia. In order to succeed, he has to pass a cunning test devised by Portia's father-in-heaven. He has to answer the two fundamental questions: who are you, really? Why are you here? Only one answer will give him his prize: Portia, the Palace at Belmont, symbol for The Kingdom of Heaven where he will share all the abundance of God.

The Story Engine That Drives all the Plays

Shakespeare sets as many traps for the unwary audience as he does for his characterisations. From a judgmental, mind-centred perspective Bassanio looks little more than a shallow, fortune-hunting fop (which apparently he once was). But if you take one small step upwards and look down from the moon, you can experience a giant leap of perception: *an allegory of the parable of the Prodigal Son.* Shakespeare always signals his intentions in cryptic ways embedded in the text – all we have to do is seek and find. One giveaway clue is this line from Bassanio. This is how he asks his friend Antonio (to risk his life) for the loan:

'Something too prodigal, hath left me gag'd. To you Antonio, I owe the most in money and in love; and from your love I have a warranty to unburden all my plots and purposes, how to get clear of all the debts I owe.' – The Merchant of Venice, Act I, Scene I.

All the debts he owes? From the soul-centred viewing point, '*All*' and '*unburden*' imply for all lifetimes and existences. This sounds exactly how a spiritual teacher might tell us how to clear our karmic debt (Samsara) in order to return to our father's true home, the Kingdom of God (Nirvana, Paradise, Heaven, Eden, Ananda) – here symbolised by Portia's palace at Belmont.

The two questions (who are you and why are you here?) are posed via three mysterious caskets. The rabbit cannot see the relevance of this scene to the rest of the play, let alone all the plays in his oeuvre. But the seagull sees.

Bassanio has to choose to open one of three caskets: Gold, Silver or Lead. Each is labelled with a riddle. Only within one will he find his prize: the '*image of the divine Portia*'. This immediately delineates Portia as representing the archetype of Soul, the image of God within. By the time Bassanio arrives, we've already seen the fate of the two who choose Gold and Silver.

PORTIA'S 3 CASKETS

"Fair Portia's counterfeit! What demi-god has come so near creation?"

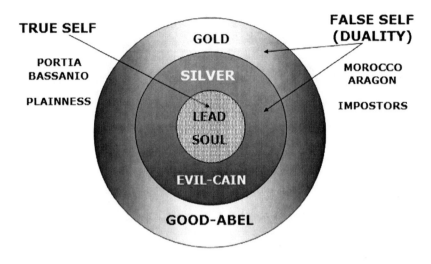

The Lead is labelled with the riddle '*Who chooseth me must give and hazard all he hath*'. It's the speech he gives here that reveals his archetype, Shakespeare's intention for his character, and his cryptic signal. It's long, so regrettably I've clipped it down to bare essentials. But do read the full text. (One of the 'seeming truths' often surrounding Shakespeare is that the text was not meant to be read – only performed. My opinion is that the depth, richness and enigma in his verse can be caught in a performance, but the text is essential to study the 'underthought' and meditate on the imagery. Opinions are like noses – everybody's got one):

'*The seeming truth which cunning times put on to trap the wise ... thou gaudy gold worthless as the hard food Midas could not eat ... I'll none of thee. Nor of thee silver, stuff of common coin. But thou, meager lead, which rather threatens than give any promise of gain, thy plainness moves me ... here I choose. May HEAVEN be my prize.*' – *The Merchant of Venice*, Act 3, Scene 2.

He outs the glamour and show of Gold and Silver and eschews them in favour of humble, ordinary, honest Lead, some of the key qualities of soul consciousness and the prior condition to knowing God directly. The 'underthought' therefore goes like this:

'*Who are you and why are you here, Bassanio*'?, asks Portia's father. '*I am a soul returning home to reclaim my rightful place in the kingdom of heaven.*'

'*Right answer*', says the father, '*welcome home, my son.*'

As we move deeper into this play, we'll see how it distils many of the parables and sayings of Jesus down to their essence. Consider this:

'*And again I say unto you, It is easier for a camel to go through the eye of a needle, than for a rich man to enter into the kingdom of God.*' – Matthew 19:24.

This oft-quoted passage has largely been taken to glorify poverty as the key to the kingdom. But its symbolism suggests otherwise. The 'Eye of the Needle' is a small doorway set in the massive gates to Jerusalem City, itself a symbol of heaven. In order for a camel to go through this, it has to go down on its knees and remove its burden – symbols of humility and detachment from materiality. In order to get into the kingdom of God, we have to become humble and let go of our attachments to false images and the burden of guilt we carry around. Nothing to do with poverty – more with freedom. This is what Jesus (and many other teachers) means and this is what Bassanio was also telling us.

To confirm our theory, in an earlier scene, the Prince of Morocco (Played in our film by David Harewood, doing a 'double foreshadowing' of Othello's appearance as the Moor of Venice) is lured into choosing the Gold casket delineating his archetype.

The riddle goads him in a voice reminiscent of that ubiquitous serpent, '*Who chooseth me shall gain what many men desire.*' Like Adam when he fell for Eve's temptation, he opens the casket and gets a shock. Here, a skull. With it a billet-doux saying, '*All that glisters is not gold ... gilded tombs do worms enfold.*' — *The Merchant of Venice*, Act 2, Scene 3.

Likewise, the Prince of Aragon pays 'the price of arrogance' when tempted by the promise: 'Who *chooseth me shall get as much as he deserves.*' he chooses Silver. '*I will not jump with common spirits*', he declares. On opening Silver he finds, '*The portrait of a blinking idiot presenting me a schedule!*' In reading the schedule held by the dummy of a jester, (echoing the words of Fool to Lear) he is told, '*Some there be that shadows kiss, such have but a shadow's bliss. There be fools alive iwis, silver'd o'er, and so was this.*' — *The Merchant of Venice*, Act 2, Scene 9.

Can you spot the two significant clues here?

First: Gold and silver are about 'gain and getting'. Lead is about 'giving and letting go'. The false selves do not know the abundance of God within. They feel empty. Needy. They need to take from the world to feel full, but it never works. Only the Lead (soul) gets its nourishment by giving from its abundance. Only the soul can give love unconditionally knowing the more it gives, the more it receives from the unlimited supply. Only when we hazard the sacrifice of our false selves' base desires and phony values do we receive the fullness of Spirit's bounty.

The second is so obvious it's easy to miss: Shakespeare characterises the caskets as 'selves'. The riddles all talk in the first person! He truly wants us to *know* these boxes are representations of the three archetypes of the self he uses throughout.

The Three Selves of Lear's Portions

'As human beings, our greatness lies not so much in being able to remake the world – that is the myth of the atomic age – as in being able to remake ourselves.' – Mahatma Ghandi.

One of the soul-centred lessons from *King Lear* is that we don't come into this world to change it, we come into this world to be changed by it – balance past actions (karma) and gain new experiences.

Why are Shakespeare's plays so timeless? Always relevant to today? Ever poignant?

Because he knows who he is. He knows who you are. Who I am. And he knows how to resonate with the Truth within us all that was created and then buried before time itself began.

In 1979, when I took my one small step on the thousand mile journey to self-realisation, my teacher replied enigmatically to one of my questions, *'Why ask for a loaf of bread when you can have the grocery store?'* At the time I was confused. What on earth would I do with a grocery store anyway? Sounds like a real headache! Perhaps what he was really saying was, *'Why settle for just assuaging an immediate hunger that will only return, when you can ensure you'll never hunger again?'*

As a coach, I often work with clients on their money goals. What I've found over the years is that a £5-goal inspires £5-ideas. Yet for similar energy and creativity, a £5-million goal will inspire £5-million ideas. Try it.

The point is, it costs nothing but a little humility to think outside the limited field of possibility produced by our conditioning. Some of the £5-million ideas are also cool £5-ideas and £50-ideas that we would never have thought of had we not stretched our thinking and asked for the grocery store.

How much money do you really want in order to fulfil your authentic desires and aspirations? What stops you claiming what's already yours in the essence of your vision?

I'm not advocating wanton acquisitiveness, but applying the principle to a goal of spiritual fulfilment, what stops you asking for the greatest result possible? What Hamlet calls 'enterprises of great pith and moment'?

Beliefs? Paradigms? Expectations? Pride?

Have you ever thought to ask to be released from the endless wheel of reincarnation and consciously to see the face of God before you die?

Why not? Do you actually *want* to come back here for another few lifetimes? Or does our culture not even allow the glimpse of another far greater possibility?

'There are more things in heaven and earth, Horatio, than are dreamt of in your philosophy.' — *Hamlet*, Act I, Scene 5.

In the West, we have been dominated by an elite that keeps true freedom of thought on a tight rein through fear and guilt. Philosophy, religion, and science are largely mind-centred. So when people declare themselves 'atheists' or 'scientists', they are escaping one tyranny only to join another. There's nothing wrong with the mind. It's just that its true purpose is to serve our spiritual destiny rather than determine its limits. It is blind to the 90% of spiritual wisdom, knowledge, and transcendent experience that our brains have ample physiological capacity to receive from other dimensions beyond the earth's lower vibration.

And so to Lear.

King Lear
How to Tear Yourself Apart: 101

'Know that we have divided in three our kingdom.' — King Lear, Act I, Scene I.

We're now going to look at Lear from a soul-centred perspective. We'll harvest the abundance of clues that let us into many of the secrets of Shakespeare's cryptic language. We'll sense the source of spiritual teaching that inspired him. We'll learn the secret of spiritual transformation from mind-centred to soul-centred being. We'll also celebrate the incomparable genius with which he expresses the most inscrutable concept known to mankind: the sound of the soul.

Imagine *King Lear* is a very intimate personal story about you. Who you really are is King Lear. Then, with a simple sleight of mind, ask yourself if the three portions into which he divides his kingdom could really be a metaphor of the three selves that divide your own inner kingdom? Ask yourself what happens in your inner kingdom when you banish your real heart in favour of approval and an addiction to self-righteous rage. And how do you redeem yourself and reclaim your lost kingdom?

If Shakespeare were also deploying this gut-rending tale to reveal to us even more about his cryptic language, what and how is he doing this?

Prepare to gorge yourself on a banquet of scrumptious morsels of playful linguistic genius.

In exactly the same way Portia's father has divided her suitors (those that would return 'home') into three categories, when King Lear decides to retire he divides his kingdom into three portions — one for each of his three daughters. He wants the best, most opulent portion to go to Cordelia, the youngest and the one closest to his real heart.

To dramatise, and set us up for his imminent fall, Lear demands of his daughters they prove their 'worthiness' to receive his bounty by declaring how much they love him.

Goneril and Regan, as characterisations of our false selves both play him like a fish. They reel him in with sycophantic flattery as bait.

'Sir, I love you more than words can wield the matter; Dearer than eyesight, space, and liberty . . . ' — Goneril.

'Sir, I am made of the selfsame metal that my sister is . . . ' — Regan, *King Lear*, Act I, Scene I.

Could Shakespeare spell it out any clearer that the sisters are personifications of the 'metal' caskets? He confirms the two characterisations are but two sides of the same (counterfeit) coin, the false self-archetype, Cain–Abel.

Bloated with pride and dizzy with self-aggrandisement, Lear turns lastly to his beloved Cordelia.

But flatter him she does not. Cordelia responds as the true self, the soul she represents. She is simply honest, she loves him according to her bond. That is all.

In a petulant rage, Lear banishes her — for ever. And thus begins his life to unravel before our eyes.

'What,' demands Lear, *'can you say, to draw a third, more opulent than your sisters? Speak.'*
'Nothing my Lord.'

'Nothing?'

'Nothing.'

'Nothing will come of nothing, speak again.'

'Unhappy that I am, I cannot heave my heart into my mouth: I love your Majesty according to my bond, no more no less.' – *King Lear*, Act I, Scene I.

When our false selves are confronted by the pure honesty of the true self, it can be a shock. We often feel a sense of outrage or repulsion. One of my own less-endearing traits is an explosive temper that can totally spin me when I feel threatened or disrespected. We all have a bit of Lear lurking within some dark corner.

In a tempestuous rage of righteous indignation he bellows, '*Thy truth then be thy dower: and as a stranger to my heart and me, hold thee from this for ever.*' – *King Lear*, Act I, Scene I.

In denying the truth of his heart, and being seduced by the serpentine promises of his false selves, Goneril and Regan, the pain causes him to rail in righteous anger. He banishes his own soul, his real heart, his beloved Cordelia from his life and builds his castle on the sands of the two ugly sisters. They waste no time stripping him of all the trappings of his former crown and rank.

'*Unresolved issues are structures built upon sand, ready at a moment's notice to be blown away by the sweet breath of love.*' – Ron and Mary Hulnick, *Loyalty to Your Soul.*

In cursing Goneril when she unmasks her true intentions as a '*thankless child*' Lear populates his invective with Satanic imagery, resonances of Iago's 'monstrous birth' and, of course, a foreshadowing of Caliban's appearance before the denouement of *The Tempest.*

*'If she must teem, create her child of spleen that it may live and be a thwart disnatur'd torment to her!
Let it stamp wrinkles in her brow of youth, with cadent tears fret channels in her cheeks, turn all her
mother's pains and benefits to laughter and contempt, that she may feel how sharper than a serpent's
tooth it is to have a thankless child!'* − *King Lear*, Act I, Scene 4.

Then, he rebounds onto Regan, the other false self − hoping (as do we) that less evil is more trustworthy. That she will permit him keep the 100 knights he needs because … because … it's his symbol of who he believes himself to be. After all, she swore love and devotion, didn't she?

'O, Reason Not the Need!'

But Regan is the twin fang of the serpent's lying teeth. Plotting in collusion with Goneril, they gradually whittle away his reasons for needing any knights at all. He talks himself into the profound insight that all he really needs now is patience.

While waiting for patience, he curses them both as *'unnatural hags'*, neatly foreshadows Macbeth's fate at the hands of the three weird sisters, and goes out with Fool to cry at the wind.

Ironically, as it turns out, they do him a momentous service. In stripping him of everything false, they open a space for the truth to flood in. This is the inner work we too must do to find *Ananda*.

Referring back to our brief discussion of the three selves of spiritual psychology, our greatest fear is that the beliefs we hold as our self-concept are true. That we really are evil. There is something wrong with us. We are nothing. The personal fear I don't tell anyone about is that 'I'm unnecessary'. It's my customised label for the most common malaise in the human psyche 'unworthiness'. Lear fears he is 'nothing'. He hangs on like a rock climber to the sheer face of the edifice he has built to compensate. His terror is that to let go is to fall into the abyss. But we all must let go in order to find the soul. His knights, his retinue, and the deference he demands are symbols of the power, love and wholeness he craves but can never find where he is looking. With callous indifference the two sisters cast him naked and alone to the winds like an abandoned bastard child.

Blinded by letting pride rule his heart, he puts himself through unbearable pain. He invests all he has of his life into propping up the false values of the gold and silver caskets. As the conniving sisters plot to rid themselves of their father by stripping him bare of all his worldly valuables the terror of becoming nothing without his kingliness seems to drive him mad.

'Though the fork invade the region of my heart, be Kent unmannerly, when Lear is mad, what wouldst thou do old man?' – *King Lear*, Act I, Scene I.

The Sermon on the Mount

Can you now see how Shakespeare is giving us an allegory of the parable Jesus told at the conclusion of The Sermon on the Mount?

'Therefore whosoever heareth these sayings of mine, and doeth them, I will liken him unto a wise man, which built his house upon a rock: And the rain descended, and the floods came, and the winds blew, and beat upon that house; and it fell not: for it was founded upon a rock. And every one that heareth these sayings of mine, and doeth them not, shall be likened unto a foolish man, which built his house upon the sand: And the rain descended, and the floods came, and the winds blew, and beat upon that house; and it fell: and great was the fall of it.' – Matthew 7, 24–27.

In this play, we see Lear playing a parody of the consummate fool. In ironic contrast his jester, Fool, is the voice of sanity and wisdom with which he vies and disdains throughout.

As his Fool reminds him, King Lear has literally become his false selves. Who is Lear? This is the existential question he, himself, is forced to ask when stripped of symbols of his earthly identity. *'Thou has pared thy wit on both sides and left nothing i'th'middle,'* Fool taunts, *'Who is it that can tell me who I am?'* Lear pleads in desperation. *'Lear's shadow.'* Fool answers Jungianly.

The foolish man places all his trust, not where his love dwells in truth and honesty, but in the sands of flattery and thinly veiled lust for power and glory.

Quite literally, the rain descended and the winds blew and beat upon Lear. He bellows at the elements as they flail him alive and scourge his body mind and soul, *'Blow winds and crack your cheeks; rage, blow you cataracts, and hurricanoes spout ... '* yet isn't it interesting how this symbolism was the very instrument of his transformation? After this experience Lear is enlightened. He surrenders his pride. He opens his heart. He reconciles with Cordelia.

What does this tell us from a soul-centred view?

Symbology of Winds and Rain

Throughout the Bible (as in Shakespeare), the metaphor of *'the peril of waters, winds, and rocks'* (Shylock) is used to symbolise the action of Spirit confronting us with the Truth.

Even God was enlightened by the waters. In Genesis it says, *'And darkness was over the face of the deep [God]. And the Spirit of God moved upon the face of the waters [the wind from heaven]. And God said, 'Let there be light. And there was light.'* – Genesis I.

Lear soon becomes a vivid illustration of the afore-mentioned foolish man, whose reckoning, redemption and transformation is eventually brought to him by one of Shakespeare's most spirited tempests.

Shakespeare's Invisible Ink

Now for the magic show. Taking the letters of K I N G L E A R, how many words can you create from them?

Can you see, for example, R E G A N and G N E R I L?

Can you also see those two daughters' names are anagrams of A N G E R, and R E L I G N?

What about, R E A L K I N G?

Interesting how 'C O R D E L I A' has anagrams of L E A D and L E A R as its primary constituents? Is this an aside to Portia's lead casket?

And last, but by no means least, have you noticed the sound of the name CORDELIA?

Having spotted the anagrams of GONERIL and REGAN delineating Shakespeare's intention for the characters, I looked in vain for the equivalent in CORDELIA. I found myself saying the name Cordelia over and over, as if somehow this would reveal its secret. There *had* to be something hidden. And, as it turns out, it worked. Try it yourself …

Can you hear the sound her name transforms into?

'CORDELIA … CORDELIA … CORDELIA … COEUR DE LEAR … COEUR DE LEAR … HEART OF LEAR'!

This revelation is profound on many levels.

It uncloaks one of the keys to Shakespeare's cryptic language. That he (often) gives names to characters indicating what archetype role they fulfil. As well as delivering a subversive or enlightening message subliminally to the audience.

KING LEAR
REAL KING

"I am made of the self-same metal that my sister is"

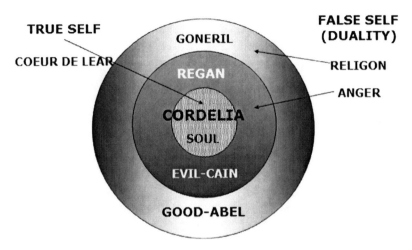

If we listen closely to Fool, he is like the image of the divine Cordelia commenting on the truth of what's going on and what Lear has really done. He's our own inner wisdom that pricks and pokes at our foibles until we listen or strike him dead for telling it like it is.

What is Shakespeare really telling us by denoting 'anger and religion' as qualities of the false selves?

He's confirming the part of our thesis that Genesis is telling us about the evolution of consciousness – that through 'religion' we are made to feel 'evil' and we pretend to be 'good' by obeying moral imperatives that are not founded on the rock of the heart, but on the shifting sands of illusion.

Coming back to the symbolism of the parable, 'rock' is another one of those ubiquitous symbols for 'truth' the Truth that lives in us, as us, in the spiritual heart.

Throughout the play Cordelia embodies the honest, forgiving, unconditionally loving qualities of the soul. In this, while it's not always so easy to spot, she links hands with all her sisters and brothers fulfilling this role in the other plays: Juliet, Desdemona, Ophelia, Miranda, Richard II, Henry V.

What's in a Name?

This is Juliet's soul speaking now. What's in a name — indeed? What is Shakespeare conveying to us by using a homonym, a rhythm, a sound, for Cordelia and not for the other two? There is something profoundly important in the sound of the name of the soul. Something that is at the very heart of all his plays linking them together as one. If Shakespeare were utilising his entire works to tell us one simple Truth — this would be it. This Truth is the subject of the rest of this book.

Who are you really? Why are you here?

Let Shakespeare help you answer these.

Realise he is telling us over and over again that who we are is the soul. That the soul is the sound and name of God. That this sound and name is 'the Word' of Creation itself. That this is known throughout scriptures and sacred writings of poets and enlightened beings through the ages as 'the wind from heaven', 'the wind invisible' and many variations on this metaphor.

Shakespeare calls it 'The Tempest' and all the 'tempests' foreshadowing his denouement.

Whatever spiritual path you're on — even no path — Shakespeare has no argument, no axe to grind, no trip to sell. One reason why we love him so much is he's never judging us. He gives us a pure unsullied truth without moralising and making us wrong for being who we are and working through the lessons we're here to learn. He's showing us all the light behind the shadows in all scripture, in all religion – because there's always more on the path. Always deeper. Always more and longer lasting moments, minutes, hours, and days of *Ananda* to be bathed in.

He's showing us that there really is a way out of the eternal dilemma of 'good and evil', not just at death or the end of time, but right here, right now.

You have a choice – to be, or not to be? Who are you going to choose? True self and 'be' or false self and 'not be'?

PART I
SHAKESPEARE'S GENESIS

Lear: The Soul is Imprisoned by the Mind

We've just seen how Lear's story is less his story than ours. In the beginning, the 'Serpent' Shakespeare reminds us of continuously beguiled us into banishing the awareness of our soul from our life. Not realising we already are Kings of our own universe, we fell for the temptation of being worshipped as gods of a lesser world, the world of the eternal dilemma of good and evil. Now we return again and again into this life pure and innocent; and before we know it, we are corrupted by the illusions and false promises of everyone from parents to politicians, from lovers to business partners.

Is this as it should be? Is this all part of the divine plan? Are we placed in a mystery school with a mission to learn something we failed to learn on our previous incarnation and gain new experiences that add to the greater sum of God's knowing of himself? If so, our learning mission begins as we forget who we really are, where we really come from and where we are destined (someday) to return. Forget totally. Soon, the very notion seems like a delusion. *To the deluded, the truth seems a delusion.* We rail against the injustice we see and feel all around us. We cannot understand. We cannot now see the big picture. We are stuck on earth, underground like a rabbit. We seek revenge and retribution for all the outrages we suffer. We find a way to cope. Maybe we do in a way. We become 'normal'. We fit in with all the other misfits who look, think and feel the same. But the price of resisting the life force within us is Sartre's existential anguish, abandonment, and despair. Pain, disease, worry, and the futile search for meaning and fulfilment in symbols of love and success. But, never mind, this is 'normal'. This is 'fine'. When we look through our mind-centred eyes at someone who is able to simply *be* their soul, we recoil like Dracula in the light of day. In the mind, we seek the familiar promise of the false king, the pretender, hoping, hoping, hoping, it is the real king. But it's not. It's the shadow. The 'Real' King backwards. Lear. The tragic Judas inside us who betrays the very essence of who we are.

If we're lucky (whatever this means) or blessed, we are stripped of our delusion by the Spirit of God moving on the face of the waters like a great tempest. The tempest whips us round to face back towards the light we have been denying. And we see, at last we see who we really are and realise we've been looking at shadows for a very long time thinking they were real. We forgive ourselves for having been deluded. And move on towards the East, the sun, the Truth, the soul. We go through what appears to be a death. But is really a rebirth. We rise up as the real king and once more rule our rightful kingdom.

Not One, But Three New Beginnings

What follows are three different takes on the Genesis story – only if you read through soul-centred eyes. If you let your mind and the traditions and dogmas of the past determine your perceptions, you will remain blind to the insight into your true self Shakespeare offers us.

Richard II is the first of the four episodes of the Henry Quadrilogy. Through *Richard II, Henry IV Parts 1 and 2,* and *Henry V,* Shakespeare offers us a symbolic account of the soul's journey from paradise in Eden, through banishment, loss of the Sound of God singing in our ear, living under The Pretender's tyranny, resurrection, the vanquishing of Satan, and ultimate ascension home to Eden.

Harvesting just the fruits of these four plays would probably yield more than ample measure to satisfy the appetite for spiritual succour. But this is not Shakespeare's way. Different folks, I suppose, need different strokes of his quill for the ancient memories to stir. And as we get closer to his Revelation in *The Tempest*, more and more is revealed.

Othello brings to life in visceral detail the very moment Satan hatched his plot and sprung his trap. What Othello feels is Shakespeare's expression of how we as a human being might have felt at that ghastly moment when we knew we had been tricked. I've been 'conned' more than a few times in this lifetime and there is no feeling worse than when jauncing realisation knees you in the groin.

Macbeth reveals an unexpected jewel. A priceless diamond shines light on the mystery of nothing other than – the mythological Holy Grail! Shrouded in the most subtle cluster of allusions we see how Macbeth, his Lady, and a line of kings act out for us the amazing grace that was once lost and now is found.

Shakespeare's Soul-centred Genesis

Before exploring the abundant guidance in Shakespeare's Genesis-themed allegories, I'd like to take a look at some key biblical symbolism through the soul-centred lens Shakespeare seems to use. This table summarises the inferences I've made based on the numerous cryptic allusions and allegories in his plays. Throughout, I've assumed this is how he 'decodes' the first so-called 'day' of Genesis. At long, long last now, as a metaphor of the evolution of man's consciousness, Genesis finally makes complete sense.

GENESIS (KJV)	SHAKESPEARE'S PARADIGM
In the beginning, God created the heaven and the earth.	In the beginning, God created the image of himself.
And the earth was without form and void.	And all was unmanifest essence – no space, no time, no matter
And darkness was over the face of the deep.	And God did not know himself and his ultimate possibility.
And the Spirit of God moved upon the face of the waters.	And God uttered his name, the sound of all creation.
And God said, 'let there be light!'	And God declared his intention: to know himself completely.
And there was light.	And the knowing began.
And God saw the light that it was good.	And God saw his absolute goodness reflected in the essence.
And God divided the light from the darkness.	And God formed positive and negative polarities so his energy could flow from Spirit to the created worlds.
And the light he called Day.	And the positive he called HU – to reflect his true name and sound
And the darkness he called Night.	And the negative he called Satan – shadow of God.
And the evening and the morning were the first day.	And as the dawn of knowing arose, thus was planted the first pillar of light.

(If you contact me through my website: www.ShakespearesRevelation.com I can let you have the whole of Genesis I seen through Shakespeare's paradigm.)

Shakespeare's texts are so liberally peppered with imagery using the metaphors of 'day and night' and 'Day and Night' (Capitalised) as personifications of what we might consider good and evil, or God and Satan, that it would be absurd to list them all here. I'd like to simply offer one typical example. This curse uttered by Bolingbroke after Exton murders King Richard II in Bolingbroke's name is quintessential:

'With Cain go wander through shades of night, and never show thy head by day or light.' – Bolingbroke, *Richard II*, Act 5, Scene 6.

In uttering this curse, as we find in Henry IV part two, Bolingbroke himself is cursed with wandering through the night with insomnia because for him: *'Uneasy lies the head that wears the crown.'*

For those of us who are more 'visual', this diagram is another attempt to represent the viewing point evident in Shakespeare's seemingly kosher biblical references:

SHAKESPEARE'S GENESIS

EVERYTHING (GOD)

IMAGE OF GOD
HEAVEN-AND-EARTH

HEAVEN

POSITIVE
LIGHT
DAY
HU
ADAM - EVE

EARTH

NEGATIVE
DARKNESS
NIGHT
SATAN
GOOD - EVIL

CHAPTER ONE

Richard II

What Does the Fable of the Fall of Man Teach Us?

The miracle of Adam and Eve is similar to that of the entire Bible. It's not so much how resilient a short story no longer than a blog is to the passing of time, but how *an apple that was never there* is still stuck in man's throat choking us after thousands and thousands of years. If this one small erroneous apple can so take root and become an orchard of misunderstanding, imagine what travesty is harvested from what remains! The Bible has been misunderstood, misinterpreted, distorted, twisted, and tortured for thousands of years. To mix myth and misunderstanding with the authority of God's Name is indeed a lethal cocktail.

> **Journal work**   This section is to ask yourself what you either absolutely believe or disbelieve in the Bible (or your equivalent scripture). Is your belief based on your own examination of the text — or have you simply swallowed some pre-digested dogma? Go to the relevant passage in the scripture (I recommend the King James Bible because it is closer in essence to the original translation.) Examine the passage for ambiguities and hidden meanings. Look and listen with the eyes and ears of your soul and contemplate what you are told.

Shakespeare, as an enlightened being and spiritual teacher, is bringing to us through his allegories an unsullied account of the essence of the scripture direct from the source. When Shakespeare extolled the beauty of Cleopatra, '*Age cannot wither her, nor custom stale her infinite variety*' was he perhaps alluding to the ageless mythology of Eve? Cleopatra, too, met her end at the venomous end of a serpent:

'*Come thou mortal wretch (she places a serpent on her breast), With thy sharp teeth this knot intrinsicate of life at once untie.*' — *Antony and Cleopatra*, Act 5, Scene 2.

Shakespeare's lesson here is hard to see because whatever happened, happened. In the mind, all we can perceive is the result of whatever caused our amnesia – but not the cause itself. It's rather like trying to see what went bang in the big bang and what caused it to go bang when all we can hear is the bang and all we can know is its effect.

Perhaps if we see Richard-as-Adam in the context of all four plays the lesson will emerge.

One of the beliefs about the Bible is that it is the complete unerring word of God. But why limit God to just one aged attempt to reach his lost children with a message of hope and a key to the journey home? Any God worthy of the title would continually, unceasingly be in communion with his children – us. Why would he abandon us to the confusion and ambiguity created by man from an ancient book (no matter how full of great wisdom) whose relevance is so hard to find in these troubled times?

Surely his holy communion comes to us every day through music, art, literature, and poetry, and even the simple truths uttered by ordinary folk like you and me. Every time a new born baby cries, is not God calling to us, reminding us, we are not lost, not forgotten.

Shakespeare too is an instrument of God's voice. Truth may indeed be constant and unchanging, but as the spirit in man evolves so does our ability to understand this Truth. Shakespeare is one of the great wayshowers of a transcendent Truth designed to enable a glimpse of the light behind the shadows in which our lives are shrouded.

When I ask myself why he wrote *Richard II*, what is he really telling us in this allegory, the answer I get is as hard to swallow as Adam's apple. It relates back to another conundrum I have often posed: why, if Jesus was the son of God, did he flagrantly, repeatedly violate his father's most sacred laws? Why did he risk certain execution for the crimes of blasphemy, sacrilege, and heresy?

I can only see two answers:

- ❧ He was not the son of God at all.

- ❧ The laws he broke were not his father's.

Shakespeare's hidden suggestion in *Richard II* is of the latter. It is a deeply moving tale of a rightful king who is deposed by a pretender. The pretender rules in his place, as if he were the real king. But the laws he forces us to obey are not those of the real king – they just seem to be!

In Genesis, we are told the same story. A pretender usurps Adam–Eve's throne. Our throne. We are Adam–Eve. The pretender rules our lives in Adam–Eve's place. He makes laws, laws that are not of the Real King. Laws that are never intended to be kept – for it is impossible for any normal human to do so. But laws that were always intended to be broken. Broken to keep us in bondage to inescapable guilt, fear and unworthiness. In bondage to the abiding lie that we are sinners.

Many great souls try to vanquish this tyrant. They all fail. His negative gravitational pull is too strong. Then, at last, the people cry out for *a soul of fire that would ascend the brightest heaven of Creation.* Then comes the One. He is the One who vanquishes the pretender and opens the way home to all. We all now have an equal divine right to full awareness of and free access to our true home and spiritual majesty. All we have to do is claim it.

How d'ya like them apples, Adam?

44

Banishment: The Recurring Theme

Banishment as punishment is a recurring theme in Shakespeare and scripture. Yet, if anything needs banishing in our world, surely it is one of Satan's great master-strokes — the grotesque distortion of the meaning of the three-letter word that has done more damage, caused more misery, more suffering even than the worst tyrants, great wars, and plagues — S I N.

Here's what my dictionary says about the word sin:

Sin /*sin*/ *noun*   An offence against moral or religious law or divine commandments.

> **Editorial note**   *Usually taken to refer to moral (and especially sexual) misconduct, the term 'sin' implies a state in which a person has chosen to separate themselves from God. Since breaking religious or moral rules is believed to be a sign of such separation, sin has come to refer more generally to the action rather than the spiritual state* — Dr Mel Thompson.

In the dictionary definition, religious law and divine commandments are treated as synonymous — but they are not the same at all! Religious law and moral values are not of God, but of man. Even the so-called 'ten commandments' and the laws of Leviticus must be called into question by Shakespeare's hidden guidance — were they made by the Real God — or the false god who rules in his stead? A false god who rules not through our spiritual heart — but through our compulsively judgmental minds?

In the New Testament the 'divine commandment' is clarified thus:

'Master, which is the great commandment in the law? Jesus said unto him, thou shalt love the Lord thy God with all thy heart, and with all thy soul, and with all thy mind. This is the first and great commandment. And the second is like unto it, Thou shalt love thy neighbour as thyself. On these two commandments hang all the law and the prophets.' — Matthew 22, 36–40.

If we consider its corollary, '*Judge not, that ye be not judged. For with what judgment ye judge, ye shall be judged: and with what measure ye mete, it shall be measured to you again. And why beholdest thou the mote that is in thy brother's eye, but considerest not the beam that is in thine own eye?*' – Matthew 7, 1–3.

The divine commandment implies that the very act of accusing ourselves or each other of 'sin' is an act of judgment. Judgment causes the state of sin, sin causes the feeling of guilt, which causes separation from God.

Therefore it is not our actions, per se, that are a sin, but the choice we then make to feel guilty after. God and man are as inseparable as colour and extension – we can never be separate from God – it just cannot take place. But we can lose our soul-awareness. The action that reinstates us in the awareness of our soul (God within) is forgiveness. We are already forgiven by God (because God never judged us in the first place) so our job is to forgive ourselves. Self-forgiveness is one great key that restores the soul to its rightful place as ruler of our consciousness. The blessing of forgiveness is not brought to the fore till we visit *the Merchant of Venice* for the second time.

Meanwhile, as we explore *Richard II* as an allegory of how we lose our soul awareness as a natural function of being programmed into 'normal society', let's keep our eyes and ears attuned to any lessons, insights and revelations that may guide us into a return to soul awareness, spiritual fulfilment, and the divine state of *Ananda* we once knew.

Shame and Hatred:
Bricks and Mortar in the Wall Separating Us
from Soul-Awareness

*R*ichard II begins with Richard, as did Adam, in a state of original innocence and divine wisdom. He is asked to settle a fierce quarrel between his cousin Henry Bolingbroke, Duke of Herford and Thomas Mowbray, Duke of Norfolk. Bolingbroke is accusing Mowbray of murder and treachery. Mowbray accuses Bolingbroke of lying.

Immediately, our pattern of 'three selves' is once again laid out. Adam the soul is 'tempted' (irresistibly drawn in) by the strong emotions in the deadly rivalry between the brothers Cain and Abel.

Bolingbroke as Abel – Mowbray as Cain

RICHARD II

"This other Eden"

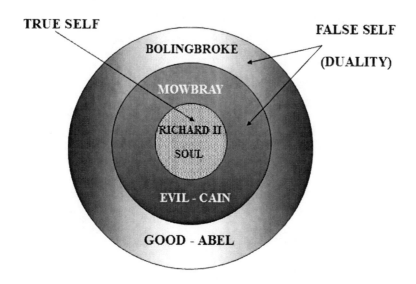

As they present their 'perfect reasons' for their enmity, through Bolingbroke's lips comes the first key allusion to the biblical archetypes. Accusing Mowbray of plotting the death of the Duke of Gloucester of all the poetic possibilities, Shakespeare invokes the image of Cain and Abel (in the final scene of the play, he invokes it again), '*And consequently, like a traitor coward, sluic'd out his innocent soul through streams of blood; which blood, like sacrificing Abel's cries, even from the tongueless caverns of the earth, to me for justice and rough chastisement.*' — *Richard II*, Act I, Scene I.

Mowbray denies the accusation calling it '*slander of his blood how God and good men hate so foul a liar.*'

Richard commands forgiveness, '*Wrath-kindled gentlemen, be ruled by me; let's purge this choler without letting blood.*'

And both, in turn, disobey the king and in so doing reveal the deeper motivations consistent with false-self 'reasonings'.

Mowbray is literally defining himself unequivocally as the 'shame' that Adam-and-Eve tried to cover up with the apron of fig leaves. '*My life thou shalt command, but not my shame … Yea, but [leopards] not change his spots. Take but my shame and I resign my gage.*' If Richard can take away his shame, he'll obey! Bad call for Mowbray, as we'll soon see.

Bolingbroke now claims *honour* (I am such a good person, how dare he … ?) As his reason for disobedience, '*Ere my tongue shall wound my honour with such feeble wrong or sound so base a parle, my teeth shall tear the slavish motive of recanting fear, and spit it bleeding in his high disgrace, where shame doth harbour, even in Mowbray's face.*' — *Richard II*, Act I, Scene I.

Now Richard alludes to God's apparent commandment in the Garden of Eden with, '*We were not born to sue, but to command; which we cannot do to make you friends, be ready, as your lives shall answer it.*'

A duel to the death is arranged.

Banishment from God is 'Death'

In Genesis, we were given a choice (do not eat or die) by one called 'God' – but may not have been. Don't eat The Fruit of The Tree of The Knowledge of Good and Evil – or even touch it – or you shall surely die. Why don't touch it? Because it was no apple, but an energy… like an all-powerful negative electromagnetic force field that would suck the soul down into a swirling vortex from which it could not escape for eternity.

We touched it and we absorbed it into our aura. It transformed us into a new kind of hybrid being: part pure innocent wise, loving soul, part lying, delusional, callous, serpent, part unworthy trying to be good. Can you now see how Shakespeare is crafting his characterisations from these archetypes – archetypes that lie at the very core of who we are?

So, did 'Adam–Eve' die as God cautioned? In a way. The automatic consequence of our foolish choice was we banished ourselves from the awareness that our soul and all other souls are one with God.

Shakespeare alludes to it here but tells us as much more specifically through Romeo. (*Romeo and Juliet* seems to be one of his favourite vehicles for exposition of his 'underthought'.) Having killed Tibault, Romeo is banished from Verona (Eden). Lamenting his fate with wise Friar Laurence he tells us:

'*There is no world without Verona walls … And the world's exile is death … banished is death mis-termed … Thou cut'st my head off with a golden axe, and smilest upon the stroke that murders me.*' – Romeo and Juliet, Act 3, Scene 3.

Not Death: Banishment

Richard now begins his 'fall'. He shape-shifts from an Adam into a very different archetype: Cain. Instead of allowing the mortal combat between Mowbray and Bolingbroke to take place, he summarily halts the proceedings.

And banishes both men from Eden.

Banishment from Eden

Just as in Genesis, Adam-and-Eve do not die, but like Mowbray and Bolingbroke – they are instead – banished from Eden! Bolingbroke's father, John O'Gaunt gives a sentimental plea for mercy for his son's banishment to be commuted, he makes it crystal clear this is an allegory of the soul's banishment from Eden, and what we lost when we fell, '*This royal throne of kings, this sceptred isle, This earth of majesty, this seat of Mars, This other Eden, demi-paradise, This fortress built by Nature for herself Against infection and the hand of war, This happy breed of men, this little world, This precious stone set in the silver sea, which serves it in the office of a wall or as a moat defensive to a house, against the envy of less happier lands, this blessed plot, this earth, this realm, this England.*'

And, to underline Eden as our (inner) paradise lost to the guilt of original sin, he personifies it as England, '*England ... is now bound in with shame ... hath made a shameful conquest of itself.*' – John O'Gaunt, *Richard II*, Act 2, Scene I.

Richard admits he believes Mowbray to be guilty as accused, and banishes him for life, '*The hopeless word of 'never to return' breathe I against thee, upon pain of life.*'

But why then banish Bolingbroke at all, let alone for ten years? His given reasons are thin, is it punishment for simply having had an intention to disturb the peace? Is he worried they may yet fight each other and blood be spilled? Or is he himself now feeling the sting of wounded pride as Freudianly slipped in here? They did, after all, disobey a royal command and thus impugn his absolute authority.

'And for we think the eagle-winged pride of sky-aspiring and ambitious thoughts, with rival-hating envy, set on you to wake our peace, which in our country's cradle draws the sweet infant breath of gentle sleep.' — *Richard II*, Act I, Scene 3.

None of the above! Bolingbroke is banished because he is the 'Abel' archetype — the archetype that 'banishes' God through feeling guilty. They are then called upon to swear a strange, draconian oath that in his breaking will later come back and haunt Henry Bolingbroke (as it does his alter ego Macbeth) by day and night:

'Lay on our royal sword your banish'd hands; to keep the oath that we administer: You never shall, so help you truth and God, embrace each other's love in banishment; nor never look upon each other's face; nor never write, regreet, nor reconcile this louring tempest of your home-bred hate; nor never by advised purpose meet, to plot, contrive, or complot any ill 'gainst us, our state, our subjects, or our land.' — *Richard II*, Act I, Scene 3.

Two words later, given what transpires in Henry IV, Bolingbroke seals his fate of guilt-gorged, sleepless nights.

'I swear.'

Refusal of Grace

Bolingbroke, perhaps revealing the drive in his archetype (shared by Falstaff and also Antonio in *The Merchant of Venice*) to '*act in a seemingly honourable or pious way*' now offers Mowbray another chance — to confess his treachery rather than '*bear on his journey the clogging burden of a guilty life.*' In stressing his absolute denial of any treachery Mowbray assures Bolingbroke; '*If ever I were traitor, my name be blotted from the book of life. And I from heaven banish'd as from hence.*' — *Richard II*, Act I, Scene 3.

This is very heavy-duty theology. The 'book of life' is a spiritual record referred to in *Revelation* (and alluded to in *The Tempest*), where, it seems, the original inner soul names of the initiates of the Christ are written.

'And I saw the dead, small and great, stand before God; and the books were opened: and another book was opened, which is the book of life: and the dead were judged out of those things which were written in the books, according to their works.' – Revelation 20:12

To have one's name blotted from this spiritual book would be not a death sentence but a life sentence till the end of our universe – according to some scientific predictions, around fifteen billion years, give or take.

But before Mowbray's final exit, he gets us to scratch our heads in doubt as he makes the prophesy that shows up as Bolingbroke's deposing Richard. Given this, maybe Mowbray wasn't guilty after all? Maybe the real traitor always was Bolingbroke? He calls Bolingbroke out by insinuating at Bolingbroke's hidden agenda, *'But what thou art, God, thou, and I, do know. And all too soon I fear the King shall rue.'* – *Richard II*, Act I, Scene 3.

Richard's Fall

Henceforth Richard is in freefall. He has absorbed the sweet-but-toxic juices from the tree of pride; and his eyes are now opened to the rich rewards that Satan and the Lords of Karma will visit upon him. Like Icarus, he flies too high for his own good.

'Perfect Reasons'

As an essential self-defence quality, hard-wired into our animal-level basic instincts is fear. When we face real danger, fear and adrenaline galvanise the fight–flight reaction. This is healthy fear. It can save our life.

Unhealthy, limiting, fear is when we react defensively not to real danger but to an *imagined* danger. (False Expectations Appearing Real.) Our greatest imagined fear is that the false beliefs – that we are 'bad, wrong, evil, unworthy, etc.' – are true.

In order to prevent this ghastly 'truth' being discovered, we learn from an early age how to lie about our true feelings and cover them up. At the top of the list of lies we tell is the one invented by Adam–Eve – we blame someone else for our actions! Adam blames Eve. Eve blames the serpent. 'God' doesn't buy it. Whatever name we call this species of lies they all fall into the category of 'perfect reasons' sometimes known as 'rational lies'. Reasons so compelling that no reasonable person would hold themselves responsible for their actions. Falstaff was the supreme master of 'perfect reasons' but Richard, as the now fallen Adam, is also no dunce in this respect. Nor is he who has now become his reflection – Bolingbroke.

The Turning Point

The real turning point that seals the fates of Richard and Henry is the death of John O'Gaunt, Henry Bolingbroke's father. With great hidden irony and Satanic allusion, Richard callously *usurps* Bolingbroke's inheritance in order to finance a campaign to, in turn, *supplant* some Irish rebels! From upon the high horse that is soon to fall, he is creating some juicy karma to be visited upon himself.

'*The ripest fruit (Old Gaunt) first falls and so doth he; his time is spent, our pilgrimage must be. So much for that. Now for our Irish wars. We must supplant those rug-headed kerns which live like venom where no venom else but only they have privilege to live. And for these great affairs do ask some charge, towards our assistance we do seize to us the plate, coin, revenues, and moveables, whereof our uncle Gaunt did stand possessed.*' – Richard II, Act 2, Scene I.

Some of his formerly loyal supporters can see his change, but have to stand by powerless as the banana skins line up to lubricate his tumble.

'*The King is not himself, but basely led by flatterers [Lear!]; and what they will inform, merely in hate, 'gainst any of us all, that will the King severely prosecute 'gainst us, our lives, our children, and our heirs.*' – Richard II, Act 2, Scene I.

53

Absolute power is now coursing through Richard's veins as he is corrupted into some kind of Herod. We can see this paranoia even today in those that strive to cleanse 'inferior' races from the face of the earth.

In a further mirror of Lear's demise, the ensuing 'wind from heaven' is foreshadowed, *'But Lords we hear this fearful tempest sing, yet seek no shelter from the storm; we see the wind sit sore upon our sails, and yet we strike not, but securely perish.'* – *Richard II*, Act 2, Scene I.

Dishonesty Forfeits Divine Aid

Richard has now opened the door for his nemesis, Bolingbroke, to find a perfect reason for breaking his oath not to return to England's shores for six years. This is the same temptation that Antonio inveigles Bassanio with – where leis your loyalty – with your soul or with your false self?

Contrary to popular superstition, as Portia will soon spell out, the attributes of (the true) God do not include wrath and punishment. These are very much of the false god. So when we are dishonest, even unwittingly – when we truly feel we have perfect reasons and no choice but to break our word, we are choosing, in that moment, to banish the soul. We are then on our own with the automatic consequences of listening to the false self's excuses and rationalisations. This does not include feeling guilty. Guilt is an optional extra we add on because we're programmed to believe that if we feel bad about having done wrong, it means we are a good person. Another brick and a trowel of mortar is slapped into that wall between us and our soul. We feel a little more desperate, separate and insecure every time.

Bolingbroke's rationalisation for breaking his word contradicts the soul of Juliet's wisdom that *'What's in a name? That which we call a rose by any other word will smell as sweet (unless your name be Bolingbroke.)'* He lands on our shores and declares, *'As*

I was banish'd, I was banish'd Herford; but as I come, I come for Lancaster.' – *Richard II*, Act 2, Scene 3.

His righteous indignation at losing his estates deludes him into believing that if his name and rank has changed from Duke of Herford to Duke of Lancaster, the oath he made when Herford no longer applies to him!

Divine Right of Kings?

'Not all the water in the rough rude sea can wash the balm off from an anointed king. The breath of worldly men cannot depose the deputy elected by the Lord.' – *Richard II*, Act 3, Scene 2.

The divine right of kings is a fallacy based on misunderstanding. If Richard (or any earthly monarch) had a divine right to rule his *outer* kingdom, as he says, how could any mortal usurp this? What we all have is a divine right to claim our spiritual crown and rule our own *inner* kingdom. This is the abiding right that cannot be taken from us. We can deny it or forget it, but it is always true, always available for the asking.

This is what Shakespeare is really saying, but of course he had to be subtle about it.

This line is a perfect cue for Macbeth to step in as a reprise of Bolingbroke the archetype usurper:

'Show us the hand of God that hath dismiss'd us from our stewardship; for well we know no hand of blood and bone can gripe the sacred handle of our sceptre, unless he do profane, steal or usurp.' – *Richard II*, Act 3, Scene 3.

'Our fears in Banquo stick deep, and in his royalty of Nature reigns that which would be fear'd ... Upon my head they placed a fruitless crown, and put a barren sceptre in my gripe.' – *Macbeth*, Act 3, Scene 1.

A few nights ago, I dreamt I met the Queen. I sometimes ask myself if I were to meet her, would I bow my head? Would you? Have you? Would Jesus if he came again? Or God? Would Jesus expect anyone to bow to him? I doubt this – did he not wash the feet of his disciples? Is the Queen nobler, more divine than Jesus?

We are all equal as kings in the sight of God. We have a divine right to make our own choices and be held accountable for the consequences. We only enjoy divine protection when we are being honest – whatever the apparent risk. Honesty means acting in line with our awareness of 'what is' in that moment. It may have little to do with the Truth.

Would I bow to the queen? Does not bowing mean disrespect? Not at all – it means self-respect.

Would I bow to the Queen? We'll have to see.

As for Richard, he refused to bow down to Bolingbroke's claim to have his inheritance reinstated. This is his pride, his lack of humility and attachment to the symbols of power and authority. As the archetype Adam, these attributes of mind with which his pure soul became beguiled, are what caused his downfall – as they do ours whenever they raise their heads.

The banishment of the soul, the cutting it off from the divine knowing and the sound of the waters, was not a punishment by God. The true God does not know punishment. It is not one of his attributes. If anything, it would have been a protection. If your infinite supply of water were in danger of being sluiced away into a sewer and lost forever, would you not seal the breach until there was a sure way of repairing the damage and reclaiming what was lost?

The King is Deposed, Long Wear the Hollow Crown

As archetypes of the twin false selves, the characterisations of Mowbray and Bolingbroke are really one and the same. So it's no surprise that Mowbray, 'knows' what Bolingbroke's destiny is in the same way Iago 'knows' something unspoken about Othello's backstory.

As Mowbray's 'knowing' bears fruit, Bolingbroke's breaking of his solemn oath and the sly, satanic rationalisation he gives for it, are the first steps he makes into the vortex of supplanting the rightful crown. He may reclaim what was once his rightful inheritance but, like Macbeth, finds the crown he now wears is merely the 'hollow crown'. This irony is made clear by Richard himself, with an almost imperceptible nod in Hamlet's direction. In this speech, Richard virtually gives us a synopsis of all Shakespeare's plays,

'For God's sake let us sit upon the ground and tell sad stories of the death of kings; how some have been depos'd, some slain in war, some haunted by the ghosts they have deposed, some poisoned by their wives, some sleeping killed, all murdered — for within the hollow crown that rounds the mortal temples of a king keeps death his court; and there the antic sits, scoffing his state and grinning at his pomp; allowing him a breath, a little scene, to monarchise, be fear'd, and kill with looks.' — Richard II, Act 3, Scene 2.

The Crown of Thorns

Bolingbroke and Macbeth are usurpers cursed by the false crown they wear upon their heads. When Jesus was executed, he too was given a false crown to wear. The Crown of Thorns. This may well have been the Romans' way of mocking what they saw as his false claim to the throne. But it symbolized something far more ironic — they were not, as it turns out, killing the Christ, but in letting his physical body be killed and then resurrected, the Christ was vanquishing the tyrant, the 'king' of the lower worlds we call 'the earth'. Satan (Lucifer) still has dominion over our minds, emotions, bodies, and the physical universe, but our monarchy in the soul level of consciousness has been restored and the way to experience the *Ananda* of this has been unsealed.

Sound Current Allusions

I fully appreciate how challenging it is to the Western mind-set to be presented with the concept of the *Sound Current*. As I say repeatedly, this sacred key to the way out of this world of smoke, mirrors and illusion has been kept hidden for many thousands of years. But if this were not so important to Shakespeare why would he devote so much time, love and creativity in alluding to it in so many subtle (and a few obvious) ways in all his plays?

And if it's that important to Shakespeare, surely it must be just as important to mankind?

Before Richard says farewell to the sounds of music in his ears in the dungeon of Pomfret Castle, Bolingbroke is the vessel in which 'the waters' are delivered to him. As he stands before the walls of Flint Castle with his (potentially) usurping armies behind him he makes his seeming reluctant ultimatum to Richard: return my lands, or give me the crown. But he's putting the King in an impossible dilemma: in his mind, Richard can only see the question of whether to submit to a banished subject who has broken his solemn vow and is demanding lands and title with menaces? Or take arms against him and be ignominiously defeated? Either way, he loses the authority of his crown. He might as well concede defeat and spare the bloodshed. Can you not see the parallel with Hamlet's infamous dilemma? And with our own?

Bolingbroke discreetly confirms the earlier 'foreboding' of Northumberland's tempest whilst also echoing Lear's raging encounter with the 'wind from heaven',

'Methinks King Richard and myself should meet with no less terror than the elements of fire and water, when their thund'ring shock at meeting tears [cracks!] the cloudy cheeks of heaven. Be he the fire, I'll be the yielding water; the rage be his, whilst on the earth I rain my waters — on the earth and not on him.' — Richard II, Act 3, Scene 3.

Richard's Revelation

In the same way *The Tempest* is the denouement for all the plays, Richard's revelation in this penultimate scene seems to be Shakespeare's denouement for *Richard II*. Like so many of Shakespeare's characters at the point of revelation, he seems to us to go mad.

'And those who were seen dancing were thought to be insane by those who could not hear the music.' — Friedrich Nietzsche.

After he is deposed, Richard is imprisoned in the dungeon of Pomfret Castle. Here, just before his murder by Exton he has a spiritual revelation.

As with *Hamlet*, when the rapture of spirit comes over us we often feel, say and do things that by 'normal standards' appear insane. Act 5, scene five begins with a monologue. Richard says, '*I have been studying how I may compare this prison where I now live unto the world.*'

In the same vein Hamlet says, '*Why then 'tis none to you; for there is nothing either good or bad, but thinking makes it so. To me it [the world] is a prison.*' — *Hamlet*, Act 2, Scene 2.

Then Richard proffers five key items of what seem like a visionary reckoning.

'My brain I'll prove the female to my soul, my soul the father; and these two beget a generation of ill-breeding thoughts, and these same thoughts people this little world ... As thoughts of things divine, are intermix'd with scruples and do set the word itself against the word.' — Richard II, Act 5, Scene 5.

Remarkably, Shakespeare is re-confirming this play as an allegory of 'the fall of our soul'. In this tight little line, he also confirms his view of Genesis – that the soul has both male and female energies. He is saying the female, (Eve) polarity of the soul was the side of consciousness that was drawn into the negativity of the (good and evil) mental levels. To 'set the word against the word' refers to the eternal sense of separation we feel by having the knowing of God and the joy of the sound in conflict with the beliefs and lusts of the created worlds. In his own way, he is restating the primacy of the Word, the Sound and Name of God, as the divine instrument of Creation.

'It is as hard to come for a camel to thread the postern of a small needle's eye.' – *Richard II*, Act 5, Scene 5.

Remember how we saw this same saying of Jesus' being acted out by Bassanio's choosing the lead casket? Is Richard now acknowledging his haughtiness, pride and lack of humility as reasons for losing his crown and maybe now blocking his imminent entry to heaven?

'Thus play I in one person many people, and none contented.' – *Richard II*, Act 5, Scene 5.

How many people have we seen him play? Apart from Adam and Eve, Cain and Abel? In this scene some directors allude to his martyr-like quality of Christ.

Now he hears the music of the spheres, the Sound Current that we only know through allusion until we reach Prospero's Isle. What possible music could appear to penetrate the bowels of Pomfret Castle except that of the divine? It's as if on behalf of all mankind, as the pretender struts upon his horse, he's saying 'farewell' to the sweet sound of God in our ears.

'Music do I hear? Ha, ha! Keep time. How sour sweet music is when time is broke and no proportion kept. So it is in the music of men's lives ... This music madens me. Let it sound no more; for though

it help madmen to their wits, in me it seems it will make wise men mad, yet blessing on his heart that gives it me! For 'tis a sign of love; and love to Richard is a strange brooch in this all-hating world.' — Richard II, Act 5, Scene 5.

Next up is a vision (hallucination or dream) that his erstwhile groom has come to visit with bad tidings. He tells him Bolingbroke has even had the audacity to ride Richard's beloved Roan Barbary horse at his coronation. The gravest insult is heaped upon the sorest injury.

The thought of Bolingbroke strutting proudly upon his horse galled him. I can relate to that. 'He rides my kingdom as he does my horse. My kingdom — my horse! How dare he?' He prayed Bolingbroke's pride might make him fall and break his neck. He asks the horse forgiveness for his judgment. It's hardly the horse's fault. He was born to be awed by man and to bear. *'I was not made a horse: And yet I bear a burden like an ass, spurr'd, gall'd, and tir'd by jauncing Bolingbroke.'* — Richard II, Act 5, Scene 5.

Is 'Barbary' one more of Shakespeare's subtle Christ Motifs — this time perhaps to Barabbas, the thief who, like Bolingbroke, went free in place of the real King?

Is this horse tale also a foreshadowing of Richard III? He lost his (supplanted) kingdom and also compared this to the loss of his horse. Twelve times just before he dies Richard III mentions the horse! Is Shakespeare connecting the dots for us? The dots that transcend time, transcend mind, transcend our philosophy? There are no dots. We are the dots. We are all connected by Shakespeare. We are!

After Richard is slaughtered by Exton *in the name of the false king*, it falls on Bolingbroke to invoke the curse of Cain upon the assassin. We end this chapter with the subtlest foreshadowing of our time to come with Macbeth and, of course, Prospero.

'With Cain go wander through the shades of night, and never show thy head by day or night.' — Richard II, Act 5, Scene 6.

CHAPTER TWO

Othello

Which Voice do You Follow?

'I ha' it. It is engendered. Hell and Night must bring this monstrous birth to the world's light.' – Iago, *Othello*, Act I, Scene 3.

We live in a world where the mainstream of our culture is a collusion of victims and victimisers welded together as the twin metals of good and evil. Do-gooders are obsessed with making us seem like victims in order to save us. What better way to feel worthy, righteous and honourable than to fight the cause of and rescue the unfortunates in life? Even save them from eternal damnation? What better way to avoid responsibility for our lives than abdicate to someone more than willing to take the job on for us?

Before you start tweeting in horror, of course there are genuine cases of abuse and victimisation of vulnerable people – from human exploitation to natural disaster.

But the poke in the eye we get from *Othello* is something far more unsettling. Shakespeare is palpating the nerve in us of when we *play* the victim card in life in order to get a payoff. When we (unconsciously and habitually) *pretend* to be a victim because we are too weak or unaware to take responsibility for *allowing* bad things to happen to us. We pretend not to know things. We pretend not to know better. We pretend we cannot see the signs of betrayal. And we get to pretend it was someone else's fault that we're the victim. This normal pattern of behaviour and the way our culture lives off it like piranhas at a feeding frenzy is possibly the most insidious lie that drives our lives. The notion that we are helpless 'victims' is the paradigm underpinning our governmental, legal, medical, and educational systems. When we buy into this, we give up our personal power and allow others to control us. And there are plenty of 'others' who thrive on doing just that.

Othello holds up the mirror of accountability to our face. Shakespeare is telling us we have a choice – always. In the final scene, Othello demands of Iago '*why he has thus ensnared my body and my soul*'. Iago confronts him with a truth, '*Demand me nothing. What you know, you know.*'

What does Othello know? What we all know. When we fail to check things out and take responsibility, we end up wailing and bemoaning our fate on the brown end of the toilet brush of life.

When we explore *The Merchant of Venice*, we'll see how Antonio, the same archetype as Othello (Abel), ends up in the same predicament for the same fundamental reason.

As you read this chapter on *Othello*, use your journal to be honest with yourself about this transformational life issue:

- What are some of the times you have felt like a victim?

- What voice did you follow?

- What intuitive voice did you ignore?

- What did you do – and not do – that allowed misfortune to be a guest in your home?

- How can you forgive yourself for any judgments you may be making about this?

- How could you be more vigilant and accountable in the future?

～   How will this improve the quality of your life?

Then perhaps make a list of the times you made someone else a victim. When you made accusations, treated someone as a pariah, acted on assumption or prejudice without checking things out or honestly considering their point of view.

Begin to forgive yourself for these all-too-human errors. Complete the stem: *'I forgive myself for judging myself for . . .'*

Brief Synopsis

The plot of *Othello* is a deceptively simple story – that also happens to take us right back to the very phylogeny of our victim consciousness. A close friend, virtual brother, and fellow officer, Iago, (for some spurious, ambiguous reason) beguiles the great general Othello into believing his new, beloved wife Desdemona is being unfaithful to him with his recently-promoted Lieutenant, Cassio. So enraged does Othello become, so poisoned with pride, jealousy, and indignation, rather than check out Iago's insinuations, he is ultimately driven to heinous crimes. False evidence planted by Iago, convinces him of Desdemona's infidelity. He orders the assassination of Cassio and strangles his innocent, beloved wife, Desdemona in their own marital bed. On realising her truth, Iago's guilt, and his mistake – he takes his own life.

Of course everybody blames the evil, cunning Iago. But it was Othello's choice to believe him, to not check it out, and to commit murder. He wasn't a victim, he was a fool. He played the same game as Antonio did with Shylock, only this time he did lose that pound of flesh closest to his heart.

'Why, this bond is forfeit! And lawfully by this the Jew may claim a pound of flesh to be by him cut off nearest the merchant's heart.' – Portia, *The Merchant of Venice*, Act 4, Scene I.

And what was closest to Othello's heart – his soul, his Desdemona.

Othello: Shakespeare's Cain and Abel?

In the 'Hollow Crown' series in 'Shakespeare's Gospel', begun in Part One with *Richard II,* we'll witness the entire sweeping saga of the son of man's entrapment by Satan and our restoration by the Christ action to our rightful throne. *Othello,* as a foreshadowing of *Hamlet,* is a visceral, detailed, study of the way the mind and emotions, join forces in us to create the mortal coil of the serpent, supplant the soul, feed us lies, fill our entire being with poison, and utterly convince us we're *not* who we really are.

OTHELLO

"Hell and night must bring this monstrous birth to the world's light"

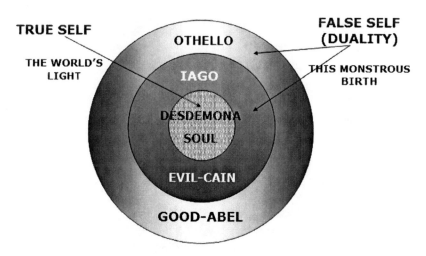

In his inimitable way, right at the beginning of *Othello,* Shakespeare zeros in on the very instant Satan conceived his plan to hurl the soul of man into the oubliette of eternal suffering.

'I ha' it. It is engendered. Hell and Night must bring this monstrous birth to the world's light.' — Iago, *Othello* Act I, Scene 3.

The significance of that momentous verse has not been entirely missed by directors and performers. But the seagull hears the sound of rustling and sees the signs of something even deeper hiding in the bushes.

He asks the rabbit some key questions and bids him dig deep to find pay-dirt: Who the hell are 'Hell and Night'? Who is the 'monstrous birth'? And what (or who) is 'the world's light'?

Othello as Abel: Iago as Cain

We've just seen how Richard transforms mercurially, with no apparent external reason, from Adam to Cain with the direst of consequences. Othello does likewise. But in *Othello* we bear witness to Shakespeare's detailed exegesis of how our inner voices overshadow and overthrow the majesty of the soul. With his genius imagination, he zooms inside us to eavesdrop on the conversation between light and darkness that usurps the life of the true self.

To benefit from Shakespeare's guidance here, we must once again make the paradigm shift from the symbolic outer world of Venice to the real inner worlds of consciousness that seem to live betwixt our ears.

We cannot gain a mature understanding of the depth of Shakespeare's teaching if we even, for a moment, hang on to Neanderthal notions of Genesis with 'Mr and Mrs Adam and Eve and their baby boys Cain and Abel'.

Shakespeare takes Genesis by the scrotum and shakes it – hard. *Grow up! Wake up! Smell the rich dark-roast Venetian espresso!*

We've already discussed how Shakespeare is working with Adam–Eve as the male–female energy polarities of the soul's light. The Cain–Abel energies function in a similar way – but as the shadow-selves. Originally, the Serpent (Satan) could only draw the positive-male-Adam energy away from its connection to God by first sucking the negative-female-Eve energy from the higher level of consciousness called 'Heaven' into its downward spiralling vortex of the lower level of consciousness called 'Earth'.

In Shakespeare's biblical symbolism the line of energy looks like: God (Day–Heaven)–Adam–Eve–(Night–Earth) Satan. The next stage of Satan's snare was for Cain–Abel, 'children' of the now contaminated, banished, soul to enter the equation and usurp God's place as the ruler of man's awareness. The line of energy now runs like this: God (Day–Heaven)–Adam–Eve–Abel (good)–Cain (evil)–(Night–Earth) Satan. We now have a *shadow* of the original two polarities of the soul, acting as if they were God. God (Day–Heaven) is contiguous with Adam, the positive polarity of the soul, Eve is the negative polarity of the soul who is energetically contiguous with Abel, the positive polarity of the mind, Cain, and the negative polarity of the mind is contiguous with Satan (Night–Earth).

How do we know this? The 'underthought' of Genesis 4, 1–5 reveals all:

'And Adam knew his wife; and she conceived, and bore Cain, and said, I have gotten a man from the Lord. And she again bare his brother Abel. And Abel was a keeper of sheep, but Cain was a tiller of the ground.' – Genesis 4, 1–2.

'Sheep' is a ubiquitous biblical symbol of the soul. 'The ground' is another term for 'The Earth'. While Abel leans toward the soul energy, Cain is bound to the earth.

'And in process of time it came to pass, that Cain brought of the fruit of the ground an offering unto the Lord.

And Abel, he also brought of the firstlings of his flock and of the fat thereof. And the Lord had respect unto Abel and to his offering:

But unto Cain and to his offering he had not respect. And Cain was very wroth, and his countenance fell.' – Genesis 4, 3–5.

Why would God have treated the 'brothers' so seemingly unfairly? They both willingly offered up to him their first fruits. Because this is not a 'true story' as such but the most appropriate 'overthought' for Bronze-Age Man to engender the 'underthought' that while God saw himself reflected in the 'good' aspect of Abel, he did not see himself in the 'evil' that was Cain.

Surely it behoves us now, in the 21st century, to open our eyes and realise that this remarkable gem of spiritual wisdom has been telling us for thousands of years that there is a part of our consciousness that can know God and will draw us towards the light, and another part that will do all it can to prevent this.

This is the biblical revelation we see and feel dramatised so vividly by Shakespeare in different ways in all his plays. In this chapter, it is played out between Othello (Abel), Iago (Cain), and Desdemona (Eve–Adam).

'I ha' it. It is engendered. Hell (Othello) and Night (Iago) must bring this monstrous birth to the world's light (Desdemona).' – Othello, Act I, Scene 3.

But we know this. We know we have good and evil in us all. The vital distinction is that the Abel-good, is still only *relative* to the Cain-evil. It's still not the true, absolute good of the soul – who we really are. Abel may lean *towards* the light but it is not the light. And, as Shakespeare warns us, unless we have the strength and discipline of the spiritual warrior, the Abel, in the guise of Othello, Macbeth, and Antonio, etc. can play the fool and, rather than do due diligence, fall prey to the corrupting influence of the Iagos, the Cains, the three weird sisters, the Shylocks …

What's in a Name?

Looking at the three selves occupying our three circles, Desdemona now sits where Richard once sat – in the centre of consciousness.

As we learnt from *King Lear* and *Portia*, Shakespeare often give us guidance and direction in the names he crafts for his archetypes. What have we here?

DES DEMON A – IAGO – OT HELL O

DES DEMON A sounds much like 'Of a demon'. As the story unfolds, she does indeed fulfil the role: *instrument of a demon* – namely, Iago.

IAGO does exactly what it says on the tin – the name is a diminutive of the biblical name *Jacob*, meaning '*supplanter*'.

OT HELL O has 'HELL' at its very heart and forms an anagram of 'O TO HELL'. Clearly he is doomed from the start!

Let us explore the characterisations of these three archetypes and see what revelations show up that we can use towards our own self-awareness and spiritual fulfilment. Our day job on the path of soul transcendence is twofold. To keep our focus on the soul within while we do the work clarifying, forgiving, and letting go of the lies, confusion, dis-ease, and pain caused by listening to and following our false selves.

As Shakespeare tells us in his Revelation, *The Tempest*, all is ok in the end — when we even forgive 'Cain and Abel' for leading us astray.

Iago: The Supplanter

'Were I the Moor, I would not be Iago: In following him, I follow but myself ... But I will wear my heart upon my sleeve for daws to peck at; I am not what I am.' — *Othello*, Act I, Scene I.

Is this an allusion to Shakespeare's intention to have black-and-white play two sides of one characterisation — good-and-evil? Othello's 'good' reveals its true colours when it absorbs the poison from his evil side and strikes out to murder the very light and love of his life that keeps his hell-like, war-like, side aside. How can a great general, warlord, and commander of armies, who can crush an insurrection like a beetle underfoot, not have extreme violence in his genes? Iago knows Othello, because he *is* Othello. He sneers at Othello's softer, feminine side, (as he does his own) and uses it as a weapon of mass destruction, *'The Moor is of a free and open nature, that thinks men honest, that but seem to be so, and will as tenderly be led by th' nose as asses are.'* — *Othello*, Act I, Scene 3.

Iago is Othello's Ancient, a kind of lie-u-tenant. Iago is also a well-known diminutive of the name of the biblical patriarch, Jacob. It's no surprise, given the will inherent in the way Shakespeare crafts his names, that Iago actually means 'supplanter'. The Jacob and Esau parable of Genesis mirrors the archetypical incarnation of Cain. In collusion with his mother Rebecca (Eve), Jacob deceived his father Isaac, and supplanted his twin brother Esau's birthright. It's this same theme throughout the Bible, throughout Shakespeare, throughout our lives. In a micro way, every time we seduce or control someone for our own selfish ends, we are as much supplanting their kingdom as a giant corporate take-over supplants its competitors or an imperialist invasion supplants their neighbour's territory. All this supplanting behaviour is driven by the mind. Supplanting is the modus operandi of the collusion of the human mind and the emotions. Driven by profound existential fear, the mind has to judge. It has to feel superior. It has to be perfect — and so does everybody else. It has to be in control. It has to be right by making others wrong. Part of why we're here is to teach our minds to serve our souls and sacrifice the base urges of the animal self. It's our only hope for a sustainable future.

The biblical Jacob, the supplanter, does eventually gain the enlightened state of '*Ananda*' and he and his estranged brother do forgive each other. Famously Jacob, it is said, 'wrestles with an angel' and on defeating him, is given the new name, 'Israel'. This name has evolved to mean in Hebrew, 'struggle with God'. However, there is an anomaly here. If you actually read this passage in Genesis, it says nothing of the kind! Teeming with too many symbols to explore here, it says in Genesis 32:24, '*And Jacob was left alone; and there wrestled a man with him until the breaking of the day.*' Tradition assumes the 'man' must have been an angel, but to the seagull it means something far more poignant. It's so much more empowering for all concerned to see this as a parable of Jacob struggling with the '*man aspect of his consciousness*' (the mind–Cain–Abel–Satan) vanquishing it, seeing the face of God and becoming enlightened. This interpretation is certainly corroborated by the text, '*And Jacob called the name of the place Peniel: for I have seen God face to face*'. This interpretation would also be fulfilling the prophesy given to his mother Rebecca when she fell pregnant. '*And the Lord said unto her, Two nations are in thy womb, and two manner of people shall be separated from thy bowels; and the one people shall be stronger than the other people; and the elder shall serve the younger.*' — Genesis 25:23.

This is a prophesy consistent with Iago's inscrutable reflection, '*There are many events in the womb of Time, which will be delivered*'; something important is being hatched here. What could this be? Maybe it will be made clear in a later episode? The finale?

The theological research I have done suggests that the name 'Israel' is an ancient acronym of *ISIS RA ELOHIM*. Consistent with its being given at Peniel, Isis and Ra are two Egyptian names of God, combining with Elohim, a Hebrew name for God. Are these the two nations separated through the twin bloodlines of Abraham: Ishmael and Isaac? Note how incredibly similar the sounds and spelling are of Ishmael and Israel! Note also how in Genesis, Jacob and Esau forgave each other after Jacob's enlightenment — a momentous event that prophesies peace in the Middle East, we hope, also hatching in the womb of time.

No convincing reason was given in Genesis for Cain's murder of Abel, Jacob's supplanting of his brother Esau, nor Iago's supplanting the will of Othello. Except in Jacob's case, he was goaded into it by a mother who preferred his smooth-skinned gentleness, to the rough, hairy first-born brother. Is this it, do you think? Is Othello the equivalent of the outcast, red-haired, warrior brother of the supplanter? Possibly. Yet, in that tale, the supplanter undergoes an enlightenment and transforms into the patriarch who seeks out and receives forgiveness from his much-wronged brother. Is it possible our monstrous Iago can receive such redemption? If only he could come to Prospero's Isle and hear the mystical healing sounds of sweet celestial music. Maybe he does. Maybe he does.

But before his redemption, his crime. Once again Iago spews forth the heartless cunning of the serpent he embodies.

'His soul is so enfettered to her love that she may make, unmake, do what she list, even as her appetite shall play the god, with his weak function. How am I then a villain to counsel Cassio to this parallel course, directly to his good? Divinity of hell! When devils will the blackest sins put on they do suggest at first with heavenly shows as I do now. For whiles this honest fool plies Desdemona to repair his fortune and she for him pleads strongly to the Moor, I'll pour this pestilence into his ear: That she repeals him for her body's lust. And by how much she strives to do him good she shall undo her credit with the Moor.

So will I turn her virtue into pitch and out of her own goodness make the net that shall enmesh them all.' — *Othello*, Act 2, Scene 3.

From the Cain's-eye perspective, the naive trusting nature of the goodness inherent in man makes him a fool. To those of us with a naturally trusting nature, we must be eternally vigilant if we are to traverse this life without being ripped off.

It rather looks as if Shakespeare is, once again, reminding us of when Satan put his 'pestilence in Adam's ear'. How he *'turns virtue to pitch'*. How he *'ensnares the soul and body'* of Adam–Eve. Becomes the contamination Cain–Abel. How the man part (the mind) effectively kills the God, the soul. Fortunately, of course, we can't literally 'kill' the soul, but we can banish it from our lives, we can die to its presence, we can deny its reality and try to live our lives through a glass darkly, through the shadows cast by the turning of the world away from the light.

Iago–Othello: Two Sides of the Same (Counterfeit) Coin

Remember this?

'Sir, I am made of the self-same metal that my sister is ...' — Regan, *King Lear*, Act I, Scene I.

Regan confirms the two archetypes are two sides of the same (counterfeit) coin. Made of the same stuff.

By placing Othello and Iago into our outer circles, we already fuse them as two sides of the same entity. Often portrayed as 'blood brothers' as serpentine Iago seeps his aural, metaphorical, pestilence into Othello's ear as does the venomous Claudius do more literally, but for the same purpose, to Hamlet's father. In the same way Claudius (and all the supplanters we've chosen to dissect) wants to rule in the true self's stead, Iago needs to supplant Othello's *rude will*. Once in control of his thoughts and emotions, he can commit any crime he so desires with Othello as his slave, his robot. First, he lures him into murder, the murder of equally innocent Cassio. From here, having already taken the giant leap, it's only a small step to the murder of his beloved. And Iago even tells him how – don't poison her, strangle her in the bed. He now has complete control over his will. '*Do it not with poison, strangle her in her bed, even the bed she hath contaminated.*' Here we have an allusion to the 'contamination' of man who lies in the bed made by Lucifer.

As archetypes, Iago has no character arc, he does not change, nor does Desdemona, but Othello transforms from an Adam to a Cain as he becomes contaminated by the supplanter's poison.

This, perhaps is the moral, the warning level of the story – we all have this darkness within, we are all potentially capable of murder and, harsh reality that it is, we all 'murder the Christ within' whenever we judge ourselves or another – something we are all doing every moment continually. The doorway to the hell in Othello is obvious. At no time did he have the common sense or the humility to check out the veracity of Iago's insinuations. In *The Merchant of Venice*, Antonio, the same archetype as Othello, gives his power, his word, and his life away to the Shylock that he knows despises him. Othello is similarly brought down by abdicating his personal power to one who also despises him. In blindly trusting Iago without question, he plays the foolish man indeed.

Once again, Shakespeare has all the ingredients bubbling and troubling in his cauldron. Adam–Eve–Lucifer–Cain–Abel. Once mixed and stirred, it becomes a writhing, monstrous birth, a Caliban rampaging through their lives with plenty of rhyme, but not much reason. Randomnicity has been born.

Desdemona: Instrument of the Demon

'Hail to thee Lady: and the grace of Heaven.' – Cassio, *Othello*, Act 2, Scene 1.

D esdemona is repeatedly referred to as another of Shakespeare's 'divine' women, but what does DESDEMONA's name itself tell us about her role? DES-DEMON-A. If Iago's purpose is not merely to vex nor kill his twin, but put out his light and damn him to hell, Desdemona's name makes sense as the 'instrument of the demon'. And as 'the soul of man' she (with all the others who play this archetype in Shakespeare) also fills the role of object of Iago's plan to have his monstrous birth supplant *'the world's light'*.

'Then spake Jesus again unto them, saying, I am the light of the world.' – John 8:12.

Desdemona is certainly Christ-like in her strength and resilience. She is not led into the temptation to judge – even as her husband murders her, she forgives him. Othello tries in vain to justify his actions by saying, *'For nought I did in hate, but all in honour.'* – *Othello*, Act 2 , Scene 5.

This is the dark side of the true honour that *is* Desdemona. This is the pride of the mind, the need to be seen as honourable, the insane, rampant, ignorant, mind that drives so-called 'honour killings' in some sects today. This is the pride of Bolingbroke on his roan Barbary, linking with the Barbary horse whom Iago would have had rape Desdemona: *'You'll have your daughter cover'd with a Barbary horse, you'll have your nephews neigh to you, you'll have coursers for cousins; and gennets for Germans.'* – *Othello*, Act I, Scene I.

Shakespeare spares no ink in emphasising the purity of Desdemona's characterisation. She is so naturally overflowing with honour, she cannot even comprehend Emilia's apparent willingness to be unfaithful to Iago. If the price were right, not for a mere trifle, if Emilia could *rule the world*, she would betray her husband.

This short exchange between the two wives reveals all we need to know about what example of soul consciousness Shakespeare is representing through Desdemona. Not only is she ambassador for the Eve archetype, but also for the Jesus Christ.

Here's a pastiche of one of Jesus' temptations in the wilderness by Satan. Satan offered Jesus '*all the world*' if he bowed down to him. Whereas Desdemona would not break her bond to her husband for *all the world*, Emilia, for *all the world*, would not hesitate to break her word (and forfeit her soul).

'Tell me, Emilia,' asks Desdemona, *'that there be women do abuse their husbands in such gross kind?'*

'There be some such, no question,' replies Emilia.

'Wouldst thou do such a deed for all the world?'

'Why, would not you?'

'No, by this heavenly light!'

'Nor I neither by this heavenly light; I might do't as well i' the dark.'

'Wouldst thou do such a deed for all the world?'

'The world's a huge thing: it is a great price for a small vice.'

'Good troth, I think thou wouldst not.'

'In troth, I think I should; and undo't when I had done. Marry, I would not do such a thing for a joint-ring, nor for measures of lawn, nor for gowns, petticoats, nor caps, nor any petty exhibition; but for all the whole world, — 'Ud's pity, who would not make her husband a cuckold to make him a monarch? I should venture purgatory for't.' — Othello, Act 4, Scene 3.

There we ha' it. Now compare with the biblical text: '*Again, the devil taketh him up into an exceeding high mountain, and sheweth him all the kingdoms of the world, and the glory of them; And saith unto him, All these things will I give thee, if thou wilt fall down and worship me. Then saith Jesus unto him, Get thee hence, Satan: for it is written, Thou shalt worship the Lord thy God, and him only shalt thou serve.'* — Matthew 4:8

Here we see an allegory of how Jesus banishes Satan – whose kingdom is not of God but of all the created worlds. In Henry IV, Harry does the same with Falstaff. Falstaff, the false god, tempts Harry not to banish him by warning him *'banish plump Jack and banish all the world'*. Like Jesus, Henry is not tempted by such small fry.

Then, in an echo of the Jew Shylock's rationale for demanding vengeance from Antonio, Emilia rationalises the (hypothetical) breaking of her bond by claiming it's what husbands do that *instructs* women to cuckold them. He even uses the exact same verb in both plays to convey the same sentiment (instruct).

'If a Jew wrong a Christian, what is his humility? Revenge. If a Christian wrong a Jew, what should his sufferance be by Christian example? Why, revenge. The villainy you teach me I will execute – and it shall go hard but I will better the instruction.' – Shylock, *The Merchant of Venice*, Act 3, Scene 1.

'But I do think it is their husbands' faults If wives do fall: say that they slack their duties, Yet have we some revenge. Let husbands know their wives have sense like them: they see and smell And have their palates both for sweet and sour, As husbands have. What is it that they do ... The ills we do, their ills instruct us so.' – *Othello*, Act 4, Scene 3.

Othello: O to Hell on Earth

'The Moor is of a free and open nature, that thinks men honest, that but seem to be so, and will as tenderly be led by th' nose as asses are.' – *Othello*, Act 1, Scene 3.

Unsurprisingly, *Richard II* uses the same *'ass'* metaphor when he reflects on how Bolingbroke too, deposed him:

'I was not made a horse; and yet I bear a burden like an ass, spurr'd, gall'd and tir'd, by jauncing Bolingbroke.' – *Richard II*, Act 5, Scene 5.

In the tragedy of the Moor of Venice, on the level of character, it is Iago who drives the action. We sit and watch helplessly as Iago colludes with us and literally supplants Othello's mind, body, and soul. As Othello laments in the last scene, '*Will you, I pray, demand that demi-devil why he hath thus ensnar'd my soul and body?*' to which Iago replies, '*Demand me nothing. What you know, you know. From this time forth I never will speak word.*' – *Othello*, Act 5, Scene 2.

We're left wondering what this might have been. Did Iago know something hidden or secret about Othello? Of course he did – he *is* Othello. The other side of his nature.

And what is this nature? What is at the heart of Othello that allowed him, a great general and leader of armies, to be led around by the nose like an ass? On the level of character – it makes no sense.

But at the level of seagull, all becomes clear. Apart neither character is whole. Only as two faces of the same archetype are they complete and rounded.

Is there a Shakespearean finger pointing to the 'HELL' at the heart of Othello? Inside Othello was a volcano. Fire and brimstone rumbling and murmuring. The repressed searing pain of the terror of nothingness. Desdemona was more than his wife, she was his life. She gave him a reason to live. '*His soul is so enfetter'd to her love, that she may make, unmake, do what she list,*' – *Othello*, Act 2, Scene 3.

Desdemona represented the beauty, wisdom, wit, and innocence that he felt so unworthy of. Jealousy is a symptom of lack. Lack of self-esteem. Lack of true abiding confidence. Lack of self-trust. The intense all-consuming jealousy erupting in Othello is a symptom of profound self-loathing plastered over with glamour, outer strength and symbols of power and glory.

Iago would know this as surely as Cain knew why God had respect for Abel but not for him. Iago could sense Othello's reaching for Heaven, finding joy, a dream come true. If Othello escaped the earth's gravity, what would become of him?

'The evil that men do lives after them; The good is oft interrèd with their bones. So let it be with Caesar.' – Mark Anthony, *Julius Caesar*, Act 3 , Scene 2.

They are two sides of the same (counterfeit) coin – neither can exist without the other. Othello, like Icarus, flew too close to the sun, too high for his own good. He was doomed from the start. Iago had to bring him down to earth. That's his job. His raison d'être.

How can I say this with such conviction? Because the Iago–Othello is a great mirror for me. I've had to learn my humility the hard way. I've fallen off too many horses and oft over many a jump too high. My body has been broken, repaired and odd bits replaced here and there. I've had enough of all that. I've also thrown myself into jobs I was just hoping I could do. And relationships I was kidding myself I could handle.

Evolution of the Soul: Karma and Reincarnation

Shakespeare writes on many levels simultaneously, with different threads and trains of thought. Implicit in his message about the Sound Current and the evolutionary journey of the soul is the ancient teaching on karma and reincarnation. While I don't pretend to understand the vast complexities of karma, I appreciate well enough the simple principle of 'we reap what we sow'. If we sow a lot of negativity, one lifetime is unlikely to be sufficient to bring balance to our soul's debt. We have to come back and try again. Because, under Mosaic Law, the balance has to be exact to the last 'jot and tittle', if we are out 'even by the estimation of a hair', we have to keep returning again and again. However, not wishing to pre-empt Shylock and Portia, we do have another way of clearing karma.

Meanwhile, suppose we ask what motivates Iago as a character to act in such a foul way? How could anyone be so utterly without heart, without any redeeming feature, so totally lacking in any remorse?

As Germaine Greer once said, '*Iago is not a person, he's a force.*' By taking the seagull's perspective, I can see a very subtle example of Shakespeare's demonstrating the idea of karma and reincarnation. Karma is an action that seems to have no reason that we can comprehend from this level. It looks unfair, unjust and downright wrong. It is a force, like a hurricane or tempest that cannot be stopped or negotiated with. Our only choices are resistance or acceptance. Resistance is futile. It simply creates more and more karma. Acceptance requires a movement of spiritual inner awareness. Learning, growth – and risk. Like Lear, we must risk letting go of beliefs, positions and attachments and the dire feelings of being abandoned and out of control.

How would Othello's seemingly tragic fate at the hands of an unrepentant villain be understood from the paradigm of karmic fulfilment in action? In a past life, suppose Othello, the Moor, had been living the life of Aaron, the Moor, in *Titus Andronicus*?

The play *Titus Andronicus* displays multi-faceted reflections of 'Othello' in characterisations as well as plot motifs. In a mirror-image of Iago's unrepentant, amoral ways, Aaron brought down the Roman General Titus Andronicus and all his loved ones. Now, to balance the action, perhaps Aaron has to live out a life and reap what he has sown. He has to experience how his previous victims felt. Had he returned as Othello, this is exactly what he'd have experienced.

This is just a taste of Aaron's nature. At the end, Lucius asks Aaron if he has any regrets for his foul deeds:

LUCIUS   *Art thou not sorry for these heinous deeds?*

AARON   *Ay, that I had not done a thousand more. Even now I curse the day,—and yet, I think, Few come within the compass of my curse,— Wherein I did not some notorious ill: As, kill a man, or else devise his death; Ravish a maid, or plot the way to do it; Accuse some innocent, and forswear myself; Set deadly enmity between two friends; Make poor men's cattle stray and break their necks; Set fire on barns and hay-stacks in the night, And bid the owners quench them with their tears. Oft have I digg'd up dead men from their graves, And set them upright at their dear friends' doors, Even when their sorrows almost were forgot; And on their skins, as on the bark of trees, Have with my knife carved in Roman letters, 'Let not your sorrow die, though I am dead.' Tut, I have done a thousand dreadful things As willingly as one would kill a fly; And nothing grieves me heartily indeed but that I cannot do ten thousand more.' — Titus Andronicus, Act 5, Scene I.*

In this light, Iago's response is consistent with his being deployed purely as a rather blunt instrument of karma.

Sound Current Allusions: How the Soul is Taken Home

'It gives me wonder, great as my content to see you [Desdemona] here before me. Oh my soul's joy: if after every tempest, come such calms, may the winds blow, till they have waken'd death' — Othello, Act 2, Scene I.

*T*he Sound Current, as those in the West who know about it today call it, is the instrument of God's creation and the 'dry land' through the 'Red Sea' of Exodus. It is the way home for the soul *'out of the land of Egypt, out of the house of bondage'* (Exodus 20). When we connect ourselves to it, it will take us safely from the prison of the world to the paradise of the Promised Land.

Hidden amongst the tempestuous emotions of Othello whipped into a raging storm by his 'brother' Iago, Shakespeare hides his mystical allusions to the secret truth that all can partake of – but only a few are ready to recognise. *Are you one of those who is ready to choose back?*

This mystical pathway has been referred to since the beginning of time as 'the waters' – perhaps because some of the inner sounds it makes sound like running water, rushing surf and bubbling brooks. Once we come to realise this symbolism, we can see the myriad allusions made to it throughout the Bible and Shakespeare as seas (Red Sea!), brooks, rivers, streams, lakes, rains, winds, etc. etc.

Why, I wonder, was knowledge of the Sound Current driven so far underground that even the rabbits could not find it? My guess is it's because it puts the power to know God, liberate our own souls, and lead a prosperous, joy-filled life right back where the priesthood and authorities do not want it – with us. The seagull sees that the way is now open – open to all, no exceptions. We are all equally divine. We are all equally 'chosen'. We may not all be equal in our readiness to choose back but one key indicator that we are ready is – we are curious, we are open, we are willing to take a risk, and most of all – we ask.

Othello is our second visit to Venice, the city where *the waters* dwell amongst the people. The setting itself is a metaphor of the river of life flowing through all of God's creation. And the play contains a number of beautiful verses that evoke the power of the tempest and the role of the waters in our earthly, as well as mystical, travels.

To get the full force of this quote, you need to read the whole of Act Two, Scene One. We're in Cyprus and, just like with Antonio in Part 2, Othello's life is on the line as the precious cargo at sea at the mercy of yet another of Shakespeare's violent tempests. Rather than central to the dramatic action as in Lear, here the tempest is described in reported speech. But feel the elemental power and force implied as Cassio speaks:

'... it is a high wrought flood; I cannot 'twixt the heaven, and the main, descry a sail ... Methinks, the wind hath spoke aloud at land, a fuller blast ne'er shook our battlements ... the chidden billow seems to pelt the clouds, the wind-shak'd surge, with high and monstrous main seems to cast water on the burning Bear ... I never did like molestation view on the enchafed flood ... The desperate tempest hath so bang'd the Turks ... A noble ship of Venice, hath seen a grievous wrack and suffrance ... And prays the Moor be safe; for they were parted with foul and violent tempest ... Oh let the Heavens give him defence against the elements, for I have lost him on a dangerous sea ... ' – Cassio.

This is immediately followed by Cassio re-emphasising the divinity of Desdemona and 'her-as-soul's' genesis in the Creation.

'He [Othello] hath achieved a Maid that paragons description, and wild fame: one that excels the quirks of blazoning pens, and in the essential vesture of creation, does tire the ingeniuer.' – Cassio, Othello, Act 2, Scene 1.

And now, in contrast, as escort to Desdemona, Iago enjoys a curiously mellow voyage. This is a perfect metaphor of how the Sound Current (in the guise of Shakespeare's tempest) conducts the soul to its source. Rather than resist the flow of the inevitable and be tossed around like a straw dog, she aligns with the currents of the tempest and is conducted speedily home. Look closely at Cassio's words. Compare with those Desdemona utters at her death.

'Ha's had most favourable, and happy speed: tempests themselves, high seas, and howling winds, the guttered rocks, and congregated sands, traitors ensteep'd, to clog the guiltless keel, as having sense of beauty, do omit their mortal natures, letting go safely by the Divine Desdemona.' – Cassio, Othello, Act 2, Scene 1.

Tempest, seas, winds, rocks, sands, guiltless, beauty, mortal natures, safe, divine – Desdemona – our true self.

The Monstrous Birth

Of all his seminal verses, Iago's flash of diabolical revelation is unrivalled in its scope. It captures the very essence of so many other plays and links hands with them in a subterranean network of hidden meaning.

'I ha' it. It is engendered. Hell and Night must bring this monstrous birth to the world's light.' – Iago, *Othello*, Act I, Scene 3.

As we have deduced, and as Prospero will confirm, the 'monstrous birth' is *Cain–Abel*. This is the dual archetype who as Khalil Gibran says, has *'murdered the passion of the soul and walks grinning in the funeral'*.

For example, in *Titus Andronicus* the 'monstrous birth' is foreshadowed as Aaron's bastard child with Tamora, hellish Queen of the Goths, easily vile enough to be the Gothic great grandmother of Sycorax, dam of Caliban.

Here, a nurse enters with a caterwauling 'blackamor child' in her arms looking for Aaron. He asks who it is. She says 'A Devil.' Aaron sneers, *'Why, then she [Tamora] is the devil's dam; a joyful issue …*

The nurse, demanding Aaron kill it, says, *'A joyless, dismal, black, and sorrowful issue: Here is the babe, as loathsome as a toad. Amongst the fairest breeders of our clime: The empress sends it thee, thy stamp, thy seal, And bids thee christen it with thy dagger's point.'* –Titus Andronicus, Act 4, Scene 2.

Titus Andronicus is probably Shakespeare's darkest, bloodiest tragedy. In the final scene for very different reasons, but nonetheless still a ghostly reflection in the mirror, Titus, as does Othello, just before he himself dies, kills the woman he loves above all others – his innocent, grossly-violated daughter, Lavinia – herself archetype of the soul '*the world's light*'. In this play, as in *Othello* the monstrous birth is brought to the world's light and does its worst.

When we visit Prospero's Isle, Miranda, emissary of '*the world's light*' in *The Tempest* narrowly escapes being raped by Caliban, apotheosis of the '*monstrous birth*', but at last we have a happy ending.

Instrument of the Demon

We, the audience, find it hard to empathise with Desdemona (and many other 'soul archetypes') because we would not be as understanding and forgiving as her. To us through our earthly minds we see her unconditional forgiving nature as a weakness. But she is demonstrating the highest virtue possible in man, the same forgiveness that Jesus gave not only to his killers but to all mankind through all time.

'*Then said Jesus, Father, forgive them; for they know not what they do. And they parted his raiment, and cast lots.*' – Luke 23:24.

As she fulfils her name, she becomes the bait of the demon – but not its victim. She did not sell her soul to gain her life. Also, in a similar way to Cordelia, who seems to resurrect briefly (if only in Lear's mind) Desdemona resurrects in time to forgive her murderer, '*Oh falsely, falsely murdered ... a guiltless death I die ...* '

'*Oh, who hath done this deed?*' pleads Emilia

' *... Nobody: I myself, farewell: commend me to my kind Lord: oh farewell.*' – *Othello*, Act 5, Scene 2.

As this voyage through the waters of Genesis comes to a close, remain seated in your gondola as a favourable wind ushers us through time and space to dark and bitter Scotland. Here to wallow in the delights of another 'fall of cursed man', the tragic Macbeth, and his reckless loss of the Holy Grail itself.

CHAPTER THREE
Macbeth

Shadow of the Grail – A Passion Play

'When shall we three meet again? In thunder, lightning, and in rain?' – Three Witches, *Macbeth*, Act I, Scene I.

Now that we know Shakespeare imbues all his plays with Sound Current allusions and how he so often leaves a cryptic message in the early scenes, it was intriguing but, even though it was voiced by a trinity of fiendish witches, no great surprise to find the above dark, almost sacrilegious allusion to the sound and light of God in the opening line of *Macbeth*.

If I were superstitious, I'd consider it portentous that today is Easter Sunday, 2016, and the rabbit I'm going to pull out of my hat is going to be how the 'underthought' of *Macbeth* starting with the dark opening chant, contains all the vital ingredients of a Passion Play – told in swirling shadows as seen through Satan's eyes.

The 'overthought' of *Macbeth* is simply the rise and fall of a good man who was corrupted by the promise of unlimited power and glory. It could easily be perhaps just another of Shakespeare's Adam and Eve allegories. But this level of the story is simply the steam arising from the bubbling cauldron. The cauldron is the real container for the ingredients in our pot-boiler, a dark and mysteriously haunting tale of none other than the loss and restoration of the most sought-after thing in the history of mankind.

Approaching any of Shakespeare's plays with a truffle hog snout sensitised to sniff out hidden messages from the gods requires one to wipe the tabula rasa clean of expectations. When it came to *Macbeth* this was just as well.

To get myself in the dark mood needed to appreciate the shadowlands of *Macbeth's* Scotland, I sat down to watch Orson Welles' ultra noir version on DVD. I'm glad I chose this one of the three in my collection. The very ten-second scene that slapped me round the chops with such foudroyant force is so often deleted by stage and movie directors. But the very fact it was so fleeting, made no apparent sense, seems to be irrelevant to the plot, and was never directly referred to again – makes it precisely so worthy of deep contemplation.

In treating Shakespeare as a master spiritual teacher, the only assumption I dare to make is that nothing, absolutely nothing at all, no matter how tiny, is without significance. And in *Macbeth* oftentimes, if you blink you'll miss something as critical as the key to a locked door leading to a whole new world of revelation and understanding. Here's one example.

It's the scene immediately before the Macbeths betray and murder the King, Duncan. Macbeth is prowling the grounds of the castle and comes upon his dear friend Banquo taking the night air with his son, Fleance.

Then Banquo causally gives Macbeth a gift.

It's nothing other than a diamond!

This diamond is not a gift for Macbeth himself, but for Lady Macbeth. A gift not *from* Banquo, but *through* Banquo from King Duncan. A token from the very King Macbeth and Lady Macbeth are just about to betray – and in whose royal blood they will ultimately drown.

This diamond is destined to pass through a line of personages from Duncan, the King, to Banquo, to Macbeth to give to Lady Macbeth! A diamond! A diamond is often a symbol of the soul. Was this some kind of spiritual lineage being cryptically delineated?

Why?

'The *king's a-bed. He hath been in unusual pleasure, and sent forth great largess to your offices. This diamond he greets your wife withal, by the name of most kind hostess, and shut up in measureless content.'* — Banquo, *Macbeth*, Act 2, Scene I.

Why?

Not only, why would King Duncan not give Lady Macbeth a diamond directly when he had the chance earlier? Why must it pass through so many hands? Why did Shakespeare put this seemingly obscure scene in? Why is it omitted by so many directors? Why did it shock my retina with such Damascan light?

A more useful question would be — what does this mysterious gesture and talisman symbolise? I asked my muse for clarity. The answer she gave shook me into a vortex of incredulity.

'The Holy Grail'!

Journal work The information you are about to receive could be transformational in itself. But the question I'm prompted to ponder relates to how the Macbeths' 'monstrous birth' as Cain–Abel (or even Satan himself) reflects something to me. For example, how I attempt to put down or try to eliminate anything that threatens my sense of power over my own little world. As I ask this, I am speared in the side by recollections of how monstrously I sometimes misrepresent myself when neighbours' dogs, say, dare to trespass on my acreage. In righteous defence of my realm, the Cain in me erupts in language and energy far more foul than the uninvited excrement on my pathways. I've never acted out the primordial urge to kill, but last week when the Hunt came through our property and we were overrun by hounds and red-coated cavalry, the horses, cat, and chickens in a flurry of fur and feathers, inside myself, I was millimetres away from the scene where Macbeth orders the murder of his best friend and his son.

The incident struck me at the heart of my inner Cain's fear of powerlessness and impotence. My Abel rose up to prove I was not powerless. But in so-doing only emphasised that in terms of changing my outer kingdom I have no control. All my true power is inside me as my attitude and altitude. The higher choice available was to centre myself, neutrally observe what was happening, and simply do what I could to protect my animals and family. Railing against the reality, no matter how unlawful, inconsiderate, and anti-democratic I felt it to be, only served to make me look and feel impotent and ridiculous – the very opposite of what I was intending.

That's the awareness, but until I'm tested again (which is a certainty) and I choose more authentic, self-empowering behaviour, I will not know whether I have learnt my lesson.

The Cauldron of the Grail

While at this point you may well wonder *'what is he on?'*, I'm asking you to suspend disbelief till I get to the end. For now, consider the viewing point here is that of Satan, everything is seen in darkness, shadow and in-reverse like those pre-digital negative transparencies, and the overall metaphor that contains the play is the witches' cauldron. This cauldron represents the shadow of the Grail Chalice, in turn, the shadow of the Chalice of the Eucharist. All the ingredients within the cauldron are shadows of the blood and body of Christ – looked at not as something sacred and liberating, but sacrilegious and menacing.

The instrument that drives the play, stirs the cauldron and thickens the plot are the *prophesies* given by the unholy trinity of witches.

Macbeth is a lot about prophesies.

The Genesis Ingredient

'Look like the innocent flower, but be the serpent under't.' — Lady Macbeth, *Macbeth*, Act I, Scene 5.

In our cauldron, two major ingredients mix together as one — each with multiple elements: the Genesis Ingredient and the Gospel Ingredient.

The Genesis in *Macbeth* begins with the temptation that transforms Macbeth and Lady Macbeth, as characterisations of Adam and Eve, into Cain and Abel through their intercourse with Satan. The characters remain constant, what changes, of course, are their inner states as they act out the new archetype.

Because in *Richard II* and *Othello*, we've already looked closely at Shakespeare's theological paradigm of Genesis, I want briefly to honour the opening of the play, acknowledge his shadow fall of Adam–Eve dramatised by Macbeth and Lady Macbeth and move rapidly on to cause the submerged Passion Play to bubble to the surface.

The important elements include:

- Prophesies and temptations
- Archetypes
- The signs of the Grail and how it was lost

The Old Testament Prophesies

Apart from a few chapters in Genesis telling us how Satan took over the mind and consciousness of man, much of the Old Testament is devoted to prophesies about the coming of the Messiah. Much of the New Testament is about how these prophesies were fulfilled.

What Shakespeare is clarifying for us (especially in the next chapter on *The Merchant of Venice*) is what exactly it is that the Messiah was destined to do. A lot of what Jesus is reported to have said on the matter is notoriously inscrutable.

'Think not that I am come to destroy the law, or the prophets: I am not come to destroy, but to fulfil.' – Matthew 5:17.

There were a large number (hundreds possibly) of prophesies that had to be fulfilled by the Messiah. But why? When we rip open the underbelly of *Macbeth* the truth splatters to the floor. It was not to *prove* he was who he said he was so the people would believe him (because most of his own blood clearly did not) but, symbolically, to act out all the key ingredients that cemented the old law together. Fulfilling the law has nothing whatsoever to do with anyone's belief. Does gravity care if you believe in it when you jump out of a plane? This is why Jesus had to do so many specific things, in a very specific way – this is what the old law demanded. It is in homage to this rigorous recipe that Shakespeare has concocted this dark, intoxicating, liquor.

Let us begin with our prophesies and our pot-stirrers, and see what ingredients the master has in store for our delectation.

Three Weird Women – Shadow of Three Wise Men

As a loyal, loving servant of the King, Macbeth, Thane of Glamis, is returning with his close friend Banquo from a victorious war. They happen upon three witches who sarcastically give both men a prophesy. Three weird sisters who could very well be the shadow of the Trinity (the sound, the light, the waters of God) and also shadow of the three wise men, the Magi of the nativity.

The unholy trinity greet them first with the truth, '*Hail Macbeth, Thane of Glamis.*' Next a most unlikely prophesy, '*Hail Macbeth, Thane of Cawdor*', then the darkest of dark calls to adventure for our reluctant hero, '*All hail Macbeth, that shall be king hereafter.*'

(A Thane is the chief of a clan, who became one of the king's barons. The position 'Thane of Cawdor' was already taken when Macbeth was given the prophesy, rendering it most unlikely to happen.)

When Macbeth suddenly, unexpectedly, finds himself made Thane of Cawdor by the King's decree, the shock of the improbable prophesy becoming immediately manifest predisposes him towards the maelstrom of total corruption. He has touched the dangerous fruit of the Tree of the Knowledge of Good and Evil. And its magnetic attraction is soon to be his complete downfall. If the improbable Cawdor was a true prophesy, then why not that of my becoming king? To be worshiped as a god? Isn't this the answer to our deepest prayer? Me – a god? Me – worshipped? Me – given unlimited power to command and control? Me – with the authority to judge and condemn? Me – showered in glory and riches? Me – without a care in the world? Me – chasing a delusion all the way down to hell? '*For God doth know that in the day ye eat thereof, then your eyes shall be opened, and ye shall be as gods, knowing good and evil.*' – Genesis 3:5.

Banquo, fearing the folly of following these demons, tries to inject some wisdom into Macbeth's veins. Expressing the moral of the play, he warns him, '*And oftentimes, to win us to our harm, the instruments of darkness tell us truths, win us with honest trifles, to betray's in deepest consequence.*' – *Macbeth*, Act I, Scene 3.

Already the serpent's poison is distorting Macbeth's perceptions so he cannot see the truth and hear the reason in Banquo's warning. Instead Macbeth, in the same way Iago turns Desdemona's virtue to pitch, twists Banquo's goodness into something that threatens to thwart the object of his lust and sparks off a merciless killing spree.

Banquo is told although he will not be king himself, inscrutably he will become what Macbeth refers to as: '*father to a line of kings*'.

The witches tell Banquo he will be: '*Lesser than Macbeth and greater. Not so happy, yet much happier. Thou shalt get kings, though thou be none. So all hail, Macbeth and Banquo!*' – *Macbeth*, Act I, Scene 3.

Temptation Gets a Grip

Both men sneer at the sisters – but when Macbeth is immediately told of his unforeseen promotion to Cawdor it implies the entire prophesy could be true. Giddy with greed and lust, the seed of blind ambition has now been planted – a seed that takes root and grows with alarming alacrity.

As he did with Iago's Serpent, Shakespeare totally shakes up our sense of how the biblical archetypes of Adam–Eve, Cain–Abel could dramatised. He exaggerates the gullible, innocent, naiveté of Adam–Eve and blackens the sinister aspects of Cain–Abel. As the Eve polarity, Lady Macbeth's descent into hell begins when Macbeth as the Adam polarity sends her a letter telling her his wonderful news. By the time he arrives home, the poison has done its worst on her too. She is even more consumed with the raging fire of ambition for the ultimate power and glory. She establishes her husband's Adam-ness by saying, he is so *full of the milk of human kindness'* that she doubts his mettle for the job of slaying the King and seizing the crown. She prays using the same 'codes' (Hell and Night) as Iago when he engendered his version of the same plot. She actually offers up a self-directed curse directly to Satan (Night). She begs him to cut her off from all awareness and sensibility that dwells in her spiritual heart.

This is a soul asking to become a son of perdition for the sake of gaining 'the golden round', symbol of 'all the world'.

'Come you spirits that tend on mortal thoughts, unsex me here . . . come to my woman's breasts and take my milk for gall . . . Come thick Night [Satan], and pall thee in the dunnest smoke of Hell, that my keen knife see not the wound it makes, nor Heaven peep through the blanket of the dark, to cry, hold, hold.' – Macbeth, Act I, Scene 5.

Here's the apotheosis of the Abel-false-self who wants the contents of the 'golden casket of Portia' where *'gilded tombs do worms enfold'.*

'Hie thee hither', entreats serpent-envenomed Eve to Adam (while alluding to Iago and Claudius) *'so I may pour my sprits in thine ear, and chastise with the valour of my tongue all that impedes thee from the golden round, which fate and metaphysical aid doth seem to have thee crowned withal.'* – Macbeth, Act I, Scene 5.

Orson Welles delightfully mocks this hapless pair by giving Macbeth a monstrous 'golden round' (crown) – in the shape of a huge square!

Thus she inveigles her husband to murder Duncan, the King, blame his servants for the crime, impugn the King's own son, Malcolm as instigator of the plot, and take the crown for himself.

Outwardly, all seems to go according to plan and Macbeth is duly crowned King. Prince Malcolm, rightfully in line to the throne, flees the scene with Macduff and seals the lie that they were culpable.

Archetypes: The Villain with a Thousand Faces

One of Shakespeare's transformational techniques is to overload the mind till it gets so confused the only way forward for us is either to engage our heart-level understanding or switch off completely. One of the clues to what he's doing here is the witches' chant, '*Double, double, toil and trouble*'. Under the surface of the bubbling cauldron, two main stories are being told in parallel: the Old Testament story of how in embodying the Serpent, Adam loses the Grail; and the New Testament story of how 'the line of kings' wins it back by cutting off its head – the only sure way of killing such a beast. It's because both tales are each entwined like coiled tails of a serpent into one monstrous birth strangling the world's light it's hard to see them as separate entities. This image of the mortal coils of the serpent is played back to us by Cleopatra, '*Come, Thou mortal wretch,(she places an asp on her breast) with thy sharp teeth this knot intrinsicate of life at once untie.*' and also Hamlet, '*what dreams may come when we have shuffled off this mortal coil?*' The image I get reminds me of the Caduceus symbol: two serpents coiled round the winged rod or staff of Hermes.

More convoluted symbology that has its deepest universal meaning closely associated with the rod and staff of David, the light and sound of God. Indeed, the twin Serpents are strangling the sound of the soul and preventing it reaching our spiritual ears.

While Macbeth plays 'Adam' to Lady Macbeth's 'Eve', 'Serpent' to Duncan's 'God', he's also invoking the essence of 'Cain' to Banquo's 'Abel' and also symbolising 'Judas' to Banquo's 'Christ' while being 'Cain' to Lady Macbeth's 'Abel' …

There's a critical moment that is a key indicator of one of the archetypical relationships between Macbeth and Banquo: Cain–Abel.

Soon after their first encounter with the witches, Duncan, the king, bestows upon Macbeth the title Thane of Cawdor, but bestows something far greater on Banquo – his love and respect. Energetically, it is reminiscent of the scene in Genesis where Cain and Abel present their first fruits to God. The way Shakespeare deploys the subtlest allusions to 'planting, growth, and harvest' are amongst his most subliminal. In Genesis, God eschews Cain's offering (It doesn't say why. Did it have an expectation of approval tied into it, perhaps? Was it not given freely?)

'And in process of time it came to pass, that Cain brought of the fruit of the ground an offering unto the Lord. And Abel, he also brought of the firstlings of his flock and of the fat thereof. And the Lord had respect unto Abel and to his offering: But unto Cain and to his offering he had not respect. And Cain was very wroth, and his countenance fell.' – Genesis 4, 3–5.

Compare that passage with this speech to Banquo from Duncan, the King.

'I have begun to plant thee, and will labour to make thee full of growing. Noble Banquo, that hast no less deserv'd, nor must be known no less to have done so: let me enfold thee, and hold thee to my heart.' Says Duncan, the King, to Banquo. And Banquo replies, *'There if I grow, the harvest is your own.'* – *Macbeth*, Act I, Scene 4.

MACBETH

*"Look like the innocent flower, but be
the serpent under't"*

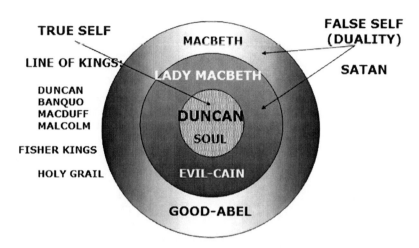

When we get to *The Tempest*, the critical significance of how Shakespeare clothes the Cain–Abel archetypes in different garments throughout his plays comes to the fore. And Hecat herself, queen of the witches, confirms our suspicions on Macbeth's corrupted nature: the original innocence of the Adam–Eve is corrupted into the eternal fear and guilt in the Cain–Abel. Chiding the unholy trinity, Hecat says, '*All you have done hath been but for a wayward son [prodigal], spiteful and wrathful, who (as others do) loves for his own ends, not for you.*' – *Macbeth*, Act 3, Scene 5.

Banquo seems in no doubt as to Macbeth's heinous crime, and as Macbeth reflects on the possible threat Banquo poses, the double-double talk prophesy the witches gave him rings in his ears.

Macbeth twists this honouring of Banquo to magnify his fears and escalate his desperation to hold on to his stolen crown. Like all tyrants from Satan to Hitler, they are all insanely driven to see 'bloodlines' as the key to lineage, they are all blind to the true royalty of the soul.

'Our fears in Banquo stick deep, and in his royalty of Nature reigns that which would be fear'd. 'Tis much he dares, and that dauntless temper of his mind, he hath wisdom, that doth guide his valour, to act in safety … they hail'd him father to a line of kings … ' — Macbeth, Act 3, Scene I.

As if anticipating the fallacy (that the grail is a genetic bloodline) Shakespeare has Macbeth murder Banquo in a futile attempt to save his crown by eradicating Banquo's physical bloodline. But, as it did with Herod, the son, the true heir escapes. 'Fly good *Fleance, fly, fly, fly.*' Banquo cries as he is murdered. Fleance flies. The father dies. And, as it did with Jesus, Jesus the man died on the cross but the Christ, the soul of man, (the son of man) lived on to fulfil his destiny and the law.

First Signs of the Grail

You'd be right to say that brazenly claiming the cauldron to be the shadow of the Grail chalice and the fleeting and possibly irrelevant passing of a diamond to Macbeth from Duncan was scant evidence of the Grail myth as seminal to the play. As we move more into the New Testament element let's open up this ingredient for further evidence.

Most people agree that the icons in the 'last supper', famously captured by Leonardo Da Vinci, are essential to the Grail mythology: both ancient and modern.

Ask yourself, therefore, what iconic biblical moment in the 'last supper' might be symbolised by Banquo, 'father to a line of kings', passing a diamond from his king *to the man who is about to betray him?*

Remember how Jesus tells the disciples that the one who will betray him is the one to whom he gives the piece of bread he is about to dip in the wine that is in (The Grail) chalice: Judas Iscariot.

'*When Jesus had thus said, he was troubled in spirit, and testified, and said, Verily, verily, I say unto you, that one of you shall betray me. Then the disciples looked one on another, doubting of whom he spake. Now there was leaning on Jesus' bosom one of his disciples, whom Jesus loved. Simon Peter therefore beckoned to him, that he should ask who it should be of whom he spake. He then lying on Jesus' breast saith unto him, Lord, who is it? Jesus answered, He it is, to whom I shall give a sop [small piece of bread] when I have dipped it. And when he had dipped the sop, he gave it to Judas Iscariot, the son of Simon. And after the sop Satan entered into him. Then said Jesus unto him, 'That thou doest, do quickly.'* – John 13, 20–27.

Before he betrays Duncan, Macbeth, in a clear paraphrase of the very words Jesus uttered to Judas before he was betrayed, (*'That Thou doest, do quickly'*) says, '*If it were done, when 'tis done, then 'twere well, it were done quickly.'* This is about as close as it gets to direct proof our hunch is leading us seriously onto something real here.

Macbeth goes even further. He also describes Duncan as a Christ-like personage, and for this reason is wary of committing such an act against one so great: '*So clear in his great office [is Duncan], that his virtues will plead like angels, trumpet-tongu'd against the deep damnation of his taking-off.'* – *Macbeth*, Act I, Scene 7.

So here is where our Grail trail begins. But it's a symbol trail – not a physical one. From a glinting diamond, and a crazy hunch, we have identified the first ingredient in the hidden Passion Play bubbling in our cauldron: The betrayal of Jesus by Judas at the last supper when the bread was dipped into the Grail chalice in which was the wine. The diamond thus symbolises nothing less than the bread and wine, the body and blood of Christ, which in turn symbolises what we've been finding embedded in the Bible and in Shakespeare all along – the 'Word made flesh', currently known as the Sound Current, in turn symbolised by Shakespeare as the tempest. As the first witch in cackling corroboration says, '*Though his bark cannot be lost, yet it shall be tempest-tost.'* – *Macbeth*, Act I, Scene 3.

Yet did Judas *really* betray Jesus for thirty pieces of silver? Jesus knew perfectly well what was going to happen. Had he wanted to avoid it he could have done so easily. Had he not wanted to be caught, he would have vanished. So what was this scene about?

As we've already noted, part of Jesus' destiny was to fulfil dozens, if not hundreds of Old Testament prophecies. Google them like I just did. Many of the prophesies, like this in the Psalms concerning the betrayal of the king were uncanny:

'*Yea, mine own familiar friend, in whom I trusted, which did eat of my bread, hath lifted up his heel against me.*' – Psalm 41:9.

Another aspect of the 'double, double' is that not only did Adam lose (what became called) the Grail to the Serpent, but part of that loss was also the loss of memory of what was lost. We lost our self-awareness so profoundly we forgot we ever had it. The suggestion we are not who we believe we are makes us seem mad. Most of us are living in a state of spiritual amnesia – in a dream we think is reality. As Prospero reminds us, '*We are such stuff as dreams are made on. And our little life is rounded by a sleep.*' – *The Tempest*, Act 4, Scene I.

In order to fulfil the law and terminate Satan's tyranny, the Christ had *symbolically* to retrace the footsteps of Adam and, rather than be led into temptation, deliver us from evil through exemplifying how we can forgive ourselves of everything that had happened in the past. He was giving us all an example of how to vanquish the 'Satan' consciousness of 'good and evil' within us for ourselves.

Judas did not therefore *betray* the Christ (because this was not possible), he *sacrificed* himself to play a vital role in the Christ's vanquishing of Satan. And helped open the way for the soul to return home.

We have to keep pushing ourselves to read the symbology instead of the history. The (apparent) history is merely a vehicle for the symbology, which in turn, as the chalice is the vehicle for its contents, the symbols are the vehicle for the meaning, and the meaning is what nourishes the soul. No rest for the wicked and the righteous don't need it.

The symbolism of the sop, then, was that of Adam giving the Grail (the contents of the chalice … the body and blood of Christ … the sound and light of God, the Word made flesh) to Satan and thereby losing it for mankind – until Jesus (King of the Jews) arose and took it back. In *Macbeth*, Banquo (father to a line of kings) gives the diamond of the Grail to Macbeth as Judas, as Satan, who likewise loses it by default. The loss of awareness was the consequence of Adam's choice. If we choose Satan, by default, we banish God *from our awareness.* It may seem pretty harsh, but there's absolutely no moral issue at all. It's not wrong to banish God, it's just a sin – in the true meaning of the word, sin. If we then choose to feel bad, then we just compound the issue. The smart thing to do, as *Macbeth* implies near the end, is forgive ourselves and simply choose again whom this day we serve.

Second Signs of The Grail – A Higher-Level Question

Unless we want to spend another two thousand years searching in vain for the external, physical evidence or existence of a Golden Chalice, the womb of the Magdalene, or the Higgs boson particle, we need to ask a higher-level question. Something like:

What has mankind lost, that if found would enable us to engender individual and world peace, and attain the greatest possibility for humanity?

'*O for a muse of fire that would ascend the brightest heaven of invention.*' – Prologue, *Henry V.*

Although we have strong evidence for the diamond's symbolising the Grail lost by Adam in The Beginning, if this is Shakespeare's will, he will confirm it – somehow. And because all the plays are telling the same story at this deeper 'underthought' level, corroboration also shows up in the other plays.

After Macbeth kills Duncan, he descends into the maelstrom of the consequences he has unleashed upon himself. He is beset with forebodings emanating from the witches' prophesy given to Banquo. Banquo is to be *'father to a line of kings'*. Macbeth isn't. The Satanic mind cannot even comprehend the notion of a benevolent, higher spiritual consciousness overseeing its little world. In a reprise of Lady Macbeth's invocation of Satan, Ross spells out for us the consequences of what has happened now the Grail is lost.

'Thou seest the Heavens, as troubled with man's act, threatens his bloody stage: by th'clock 'tis day, and yet dark Night [Satan] strangles the travelling lamp: is't Night's [Satan's] predominance, or the Day's [God's] shame, that Darkness does the face of Earth entomb, when living Light should kiss it?' – Macbeth, Act 2, Scene 4.

Compare now these two parallels between Richard and Macbeth in their roles as Adam.

'Show us the hand of God that hath dismiss'd us from our stewardship; for well we know no hand of blood and bone can gripe the sacred handle of our sceptre, unless he do profane, steal or usurp.' – Richard II, Act 3, Scene 3.

'Our fears in Banquo stick deep, and in his royalty of Nature reigns that which would be fear'd ... Upon my head they placed a fruitless crown, and put a barren sceptre in my gripe ... ' – Macbeth, Act 3, Scene I.

This soliloquy continues with the (not so hidden) gem we badly need to corroborate our hypothesis that the diamond is indeed a sign of the Grail:

' ... *Thence to be wrench'd with an unlineal hand, no son of mine succeeding: if't be so, for Banquo's issue have I fil'd my mind, for them, the gracious Duncan have I murther'd, put rancours in the vessel of my peace only for them, and mine eternal jewel given to the common enemy of man, to make them Kings, the sons of Banquo Kings. Rather than so, come Fate into the list, and champion me to th' utterance.'* — Macbeth, Act 3, Scene I.

Right here we're delving into the genesis of how the negative force, *the common enemy of man*, got its power to compulsively dominate, exterminate, take over all opposition and competition and commit with impunity all manner of atrocity, and inhuman acts of callous indifference.

Right here we find the hidden gem that links the mysterious appearance of that priceless diamond to something lost by Adam when he tasted the sweet promise of unlimited power and glory.

You may already have spotted it. But hold your horses for a second. Earlier, we asked, 'what has mankind lost that, if we found it, would restore us to our full potential as human beings?'.

Right Here Shakespeare Tells Us What This Is

When Macbeth laments how he lost *'mine eternal jewel given to the common enemy of man'* is he alluding to the diamond, the soul, the Grail, lost to Satan, *the common enemy of man*, in the beginning? Is this the Sound of the waters, the *'wind from heaven'* Shakespeare has playing in the background in all his plays until he finally lets it rise to the surface in his finale, *The Tempest*?

Is this the 'jewel' reclaimed for all mankind by Jesus Christ when he vanquished Satan at the resurrection?

Will these iconic symbols and double-symbols of symbols of symbols continue to bubble to the surface as we change our focus more towards the New Testament ingredients? Let me count the ways. Simmering in the sub-text, as well as the betrayal by Judas, all these iconic prophesies are alluded to and fulfilled:

BIBLICAL MOTIF	SHAKESPEARE MOTIF
Sound and light of God (The Word, the Sound Current).	Thunder, lightning, and rain.
Three wise men.	Three weird women.
Chalice of the Eucharist.	Cauldron of the Grail.
Serpent tempts Adam through Eve – The Fall of Man.	Prophesy: Macbeth will be king – Lady Macbeth incites him to murder .
Prophesies of the Messiah.	Prophesy: Banquo will be *'father to a line of kings'.*
Christ passes bread and wine to Judas.	Banquo passes diamond to Macbeth.
The gates of hell shall not prevail.	Macduff's knocking on gates of castle.
The Crown of Thorns and the sign INRI.	Macbeth fruitless crown – barren sceptre.
Death and resurrection of Christ.	Death and rising of Banquo as ghost.
Herod's massacre of the innocents.	Macbeth slaughters Macduff's babies.
Blood of Christ washes clean the sins.	Liver of blaspheming Jew.
Virgin birth of Jesus.	Macduff 'not of woman born'.
Christ bears the cross to Calvary Hill.	Malcolm bears Burnam Wood to Dunsinane Hill.
Harrowing of Hell.	Macbeth killed offstage.
Satan vanquished by the real king.	Macduff slays Macbeth.
Christ takes the sin of the world.	Malcolm's confession of great lust.
Pilate washes his hands of Jesus' blood.	Lady Macbeth obsessively washes her hands.
The comforter of Pentecost.	The comfort of Macbeth's severed head.

Nail That Grail

If we want *Macbeth* to be a serious contender for having the last word on the Grail, let's discern myth from reality and nail that Grail for good.

The Holy Grail has two dictionary definitions:

1   In medieval legend, the cup or platter used by Christ at the Last Supper, and in which Joseph of Arimathea received Christ's blood at the Cross. Quests for it undertaken by medieval knights are described in versions of the Arthurian legends written from the early 13th century onward.

2   A thing which is eagerly pursued or sought after.

More recently, thanks to the 'forensic' research of Leigh, Baigent, and Lincoln in *Holy Blood Holy Grail*, sensationalised by Dan Brown's blockbusting *The Da Vinci Code*, it now has a third (albeit speculative) definition as: *the bloodline of Jesus Christ*. This is presumed to be subsequent to his marriage to and children with Mary Magdalene. Which in turn presumes he survived the crucifixion.

How could such leaps of fantasy slipstream so naturally in the zeitgeist? Because on some level it's true. But between truth and the criteria of scientific proof is a gap many light years wide. However, behind the shadows demanding physical evidence that makes logical sense before declaring things as true – there is a light.

Shakespeare's Revelation offers mankind a fresh look at this ancient mystery and a new way to understand it unsullied by dogma and religious politics. When he wrote *The Tempest* and all the tempests in its brewing, he was not only telling mankind about the divine instrument of all creation, but also the ultimate revelation of what the *Holy Grail* really is.

The Grail Trail Beyond Da Vinci

Given there's a possible Truth inherent in *The Da Vinci Code* let us get to the root of the deeper meaning. Could the assumed '*bloodline of Jesus*' itself be a symbol of something far deeper and more significant?

Brown's Grail trail seemed to stop at Rosslyn Chapel – not far from Dunsinane. Then right at the end of the book we were left wondering if the 'womb of the Magdalene' was actually in her body buried under the Louvre! We'll never know. What we do know, based on the fires it ignited in vast swathes of us, is there is something about this idea of a 'bloodline of Christ' that harmonises with some deep inner knowing. What?

In the book *Holy Blood Holy Grail* Leigh, Baigent and Lincoln became convinced that 'Holy Grail' was originally pronounced Sang Graal, a homonym of Sang Real meaning Royal Blood.

Then to make sense of this from a mind-centred, secular perspective they had little alternative but to speculate that Jesus must have survived the crucifixion, married Mary Magdalene, and sired a secret dynasty. There are paintings on the walls of the chapel at Rennes le Château that can be interpreted to corroborate this notion.

Whatever the Truth, something about this fable has driven millions of folk crazy for centuries.

Once again Jesus is the key ingredient in the cauldron. What does he say about his own blood?

Looking at the last supper again Matthew said, '*And as they were eating, Jesus took bread, and blessed it, and brake it, and gave it to the disciples, and said, Take, eat; this is my body. And he took the cup, and gave thanks, and gave it to them, saying, Drink ye all of it; For this is my blood of the new testament, which is shed for many for the remission of sins.*' – Matthew 26:27.

The symbol trail here is very deeply convoluted but, if you want to understand this stuff, really worth stretching your mind round. In saying that 'bread' symbolises his body, Jesus is saying bread in turn symbolises the 'Word made flesh'. The Word, while its vibration does translate down to the body of Jesus, as much as it does our own, really relates to the sacred Name (sound, voice) of God. This is what we refer to as the Sound Current. The phrase *'my blood of the new testament'* means the spiritual promise of the New Testament, the promised liberation of the soul, was sealed in his blood which in turn is a symbol for the Holy Spirit, the Light of God. This means that promise is as absolutely rock solid as it gets. Thy will is done.

Jesus called himself many symbolic things, including as Shakespeare likes to remind us: *'the light of the world'*.

'Then spake Jesus again unto them, saying, I am the light of the world: he that followeth me shall not walk in darkness, but shall have the light of life.' – John 8:12.

Putting all this together, true holy communion occurs when the 'bread and the wine' come together – when 'The Sound of The Name converges with The Light of the Soul'. Any one of us can partake of authentic holy communion at any moment we choose – and while a priest or 'intermediary' may facilitate this, it is something we have to do for ourselves anyway. All we have to do is ask for the Light for the highest good, call the Name and it is done. The Grail is fully present as us, in us, in the now, in the Sabbath moment. The good news is it is present, here, now. The bad news is, as Lorenzo tells Jessica, through the physical senses *'this muddy vesture of decay'* we cannot conceive it or hear it – because the mind is not in the present, it is either in the past or in the future, neither of which exist at all. This is why anything that satisfies the mind cannot possibly be the Truth. And anything that is the Truth will be rejected by the temporal demands of the mortal mind.

107

Macbeth's Strange Encounter of the Second Time

Jauncing ahead to Act Four, anticipating Macbeth's reappearance, the three weird women concoct a new brew and cast their spells. Some of these substances may simply be seasoning, but the meat of the matter is represented by two dark ingredients. What does your inner sleuth smell rising in the steam?

'Round about the cauldron go: in the poison'd entrails throw. Toad, that under cold stone days and nights, has thirty one: swelter'd venom sleeping got, boil Thou first i'th'charmed pot.

'Double, double toil and trouble, Fire burn, and cauldron bubble. Fillet of a fenny snake, in the cauldron boil and bake. Eye of newt and toe of frog, Wool of bat and tongue of dog, Adder's fork and blind-worm's sting, Lizard's leg and owlet's wing, For a charm of powerful trouble, Like a hell-broth boil and bubble.

'Double, double toil and trouble, Fire burn and cauldron bubble. Scale of dragon, tooth of wolf, Witches' mummy, maw and gulf Of the ravined salt-sea shark, Root of hemlock digged i' th' dark, Liver of blaspheming Jew, Gall of goat and slips of yew Slivered in the moon's eclipse, Nose of Turk and Tartar's lips, Finger of birth-strangled babe Ditch-delivered by a drab, Make the gruel thick and slab. Add thereto a tiger's chaudron, For the ingredients of our cauldron.

'Double, double toil and trouble, fire burn and cauldron bubble. Cool it with a baboon's blood, Then the charm is firm and good.' – Macbeth, Act 4, Scene 1.

The dark trinity of ingredients that jumped right out at me and gave me that 'diamond feeling' were: *'Fillet of a fenny snake', 'Adder's fork,'* and *'Liver of blaspheming Jew'*!

Poison, venom, a snake and an adder's fork must surely be an allusion to the toxic effects of Satan and the twin Serpents. But where does the Blaspheming Jew fit in?

Jesus, King of the Jews, had a penchant for poking the Sanhedrin Bear.

'If ye had known me, ye should have known my Father also: and from henceforth ye know him, and have seen him.' — John 14:7.

'Again the high priest asked him, and said unto him, Art Thou the Christ, the Son of the Blessed? And Jesus said, I am: and ye shall see the Son of man sitting on the right hand of power, and coming in the clouds of heaven. Then the high priest rent his clothes, and saith, What need we any further witnesses?' — Mark 14:61

In other words, he was claiming to be one with God. Although Jesus most probably meant that at the level of soul, we are all sons of God, this was certainly not understood at the time and in the eyes of the Sanhedrin, made him unequivocally guilty of blasphemy — for which the sentence was death (probably by stoning).

Is Shakespeare then daring to refer to Jesus Christ as the 'Blaspheming Jew'. If not, who else? If so, the most important ingredient in the cauldron — and thus the entire play — would be Jesus Christ. This remains to be seen. And seen it will be.

But if this is so, why is only the liver flung into the chalice? Why not the heart, brain or stomach?

Because, presumably, the liver is the organ that takes the toxins out of the blood and cleanses it. In this way 'the liver of blaspheming Jew' becomes a metaphor for the Christ action of 'taking the sin of the world and cleansing it through his own blood'? Something else he told us about in his typically cryptic way at the iconic 'last supper'.

From Satan's perspective, this is the last thing he wants to have happen. From his perspective he is the god of all the world. To him Jesus would be a liar, a blaspheming Jew who claims to be as God and must die for his audacity.

The reformation did open up new freedoms of thought but I'm not sure how comfortably this line of thought will be swallowed now – let alone back in Shakespeare's day.

Terminally vexed Macbeth now unwisely seeks further guidance from the three weird women. Invoking a tempestuous Sound Current allusion, he demands answers:

'Though you untie the winds, and let them fight against the churches: though the yesty waves confound and swallow navigation up . . . answer me to what I ask you.' – Macbeth, Act 4, Scene I.

How many facets of the Grail diamond can you see glinting through the shadows of their answer?

Once again they play him like a cheap set of bagpipes. They show him three apparitions who equally taunt and jibe at him with more double-talk. He now gets the prophesy that ensures his downfall by playing to the delusion of all the demi-gods – almighty power.

Each heralded by the 'Shadow Sound Current' of thunder, the first of three apparitions, an Armed Head, warns him *'Macbeth! Macbeth! Macbeth! Beware Macduff. Beware the thane of Fife. Dismiss me. Enough.'*

The second apparition, a 'bloody child', appears and allays his fears, *'Macbeth, Macbeth, Macbeth'*, it chants his name three times. Macbeth emphasises this, *'Had I three ears, I'd hear thee.'*

'Be bloody, bold and resolute:, it continues, *'laugh to scorn the power of man; for none of woman born shall harm Macbeth.'*

This is a delicious shadow of the Old Testament prophesy that the Messiah would be 'of a virgin born'.

'*Therefore the Lord himself shall give you a sign; Behold, a virgin shall conceive, and bear a son, and shall call his name Immanuel.*' Isaiah 7:14.

Finally, the 'Sound' heralds the third apparition: a Child crowned, with a tree in his hand. Macbeth howls, '*What is this that rises like the issue of a King, and wears upon his baby-brow, the round and top of sovereignty?*' The birth, death and resurrection of the Christ, I would venture. Specifically the tree hewn from Burnham Wood to represent the cross upon which not Christ, but ironically, Satan's tyranny was terminated.

And the 'child' counsels him, '*Be lion-mettled, proud and take no care: who chafes, who frets, or where conspirators are: Macbeth shall never vanquished be until Great Birnam Wood, to high Dunsinane Hill shall come against him.*' — Macbeth, Act 4, Scene I.

Here we have the prophesy that Satan will be vanquished when the Christ bears the wooden cross out of the gates of Jerusalem (the holy city — symbol of God's kingdom) to Calvary Hill, and seals the New Testament in his own blood.

Nevertheless, Macbeth, despite being over confident in his powers, takes no chances and, like Herod in Bethlehem, like the Dauphin at Agincourt, gives the Satanic command to '*massacre the innocents*' and wipe out Macduff's bloodline (plus an explicit nod to the spiritual line we've been discussing), '*Give to the' edge o' th' sword his wife, his babes, and all unfortunate souls that trace him in his line.*' — Macbeth, Act 4, Scene I.

Just as they did on his first encounter, the witches give him one direct prophesy followed by two cryptic truths destined to have him hoist by his own petard. Satan lied to Eve by giving her a false promise couched in words that only seem true once she had fallen into his delusion.

'*And the serpent said unto the woman, ye shall not surely die: For God doth know that in the day ye eat thereof, then your eyes shall be opened, and ye shall be as gods, knowing good and evil.*' — Genesis 3:4.

The witches did not lie to Macbeth, but led him into temptation where his arrogance would make him delude himself and become vulnerable to the sword of the spiritual warrior, Thane of Fife, Macduff.

This vanquishing of Satan was foreshadowed in Act Two immediately after the murder of Duncan, just before the crime was discovered. There is a persistent knocking at the gates of his castle. Knocking is one of the sounds of the Sound Current and who should it be knocking and demanding entry – Macduff.

'And I say also unto thee, That Thou art Peter, and upon this rock [the Name and Sound of God] I will build my church; and the gates of hell shall not prevail against it.' – Matthew 16:18

Final Curtain

To complete the shining of our spotlight into the shadows of this Passion Play, not in any chronological order, there are six final iconic motifs to illuminate.

- Pontius Pilate Washes his hands

- Jesus forgives all mankind

- Christ takes the sin of the world

- The Virgin Birth

- Vanquishing of Satan and 'Harrowing of hell'

- Pentecost – the coming of the comforter

Lady Macbeth Cannot Wash Clean Her Hands

Lest we forget our tragic anti-heroine, Eve, played by Lady Macbeth, she contributes two major ingredients to our boiling pot. In the light of our hidden theme, the bizarre scenes of her obsessive-compulsive hand-washing behaviour take on new significance.

'Out, damned spot! Out, I say! — One, two. Why, then, 'tis time to do 't. Hell is murky! — Fie, my lord, fie! A soldier, and afeard? What need we fear who knows it, when none can call our power to account? — Yet who would have thought the old man to have had so much blood in him ... Here's the smell of the blood still. All the perfumes of Arabia will not sweeten this little hand. Oh, Oh, Oh!' — Macbeth, Act 5, Scene 1.

Who in the scripture infamously washes his hands of the blood of Christ?

Pontius Pilate.

Pilate knew Jesus to be innocent, yet allowed the Sanhedrin to execute him in the cruellest possible Roman way. Is this Shakespeare's shadowy way of indicting him in the crime? Or perhaps indicting us every time we allow evil to prosper by doing nothing?

Malcolm Takes the 'Sin of the World'

'The next day John seeth Jesus coming unto him, and saith, Behold the Lamb of God, which taketh away the sin of the world.' — John 1:29.

Just before the final assault on the Gates of Hell, 'high Dunsinane Hill', as if smitten by a mysterious virus, Malcolm is struck by an overbearing burden of shame.

On the cross, Jesus took this burden to himself. He experienced all the negativity of the world and transmuted it to love through forgiveness. In his overcoming of the world, he transformed human consciousness back into having the freedom of choice we had in the Garden of Eden. He did this for all humanity. It was just done. It is done. Regardless of religion, race, colour or sexual preference.

There's no need to believe any of this. All you need to do is check it out for yourself. If you're drawn to check it out, it means you're probably ready. If you're not, you're probably not. It really is that simple. How you check it out is up to you.

Likewise, Malcolm as the Christ, takes upon himself the 'sin of the world'. Seemingly racked with doubt as to his right to rule Scotland, Malcolm staggers Macduff (and us) by confessing to an exhaustive litany of apparent sins that makes Macbeth look like Mother Theresa.

'When I shall tread upon the tyrant's head, or wear it on my sword, yet my poor country shall have more vices than it had before, more suffer, and more sundry ways than ever, by him that shall succeed.' — Macbeth, Act 4, Scene 3.

'What should he be?' questions Macduff.

'It is myself I mean, in whom I know all the particulars of vice so grafted, that when they shall be open'd, black Macbeth will seem pure as snow, and the poor State esteem him as a lamb, being compar'd with my confineless harms.'

Macduff retorts with, *'Not in the legions of horrid hell can come a devil more damned in evils to top Macbeth.'*

'I grant him bloody, luxurious, avaricious, false, deceitful, sudden, malicious, smacking of every sin that has a name. But there's no bottom, none, in my voluptuousness. Your wives, your daughters, your matrons, and your maids could not fill up the cistern of my lust, and my desire all continent impediments would o'erbear that did oppose my will. Better Macbeth than such an one to reign.'

Understandably, Macduff is utterly dismayed and, as was Jesus accused, accuses Malcolm of blasphemy, *'Since that the truest issue of thy Throne by his own interdictions stands accus'd, and does blaspheme his breed ... These evils thou repeat'st upon thyself, have banish'd me from Scotland. O my breast, thy hope ends here.'*

Shakespeare gives us no respite – the motifs come at us off the stage like a hail of bullets. Here we receive just enough of the trial of Jesus to make sure all the key ingredients are accounted for.

But the very confession by Malcolm of his 'sins', immediately clears them from his consciousness allowing the concluding events to unfold.

'Macduff, this noble passion, Child of integrity, hath from my soul wip'd the black scruples, reconcil'd my thoughts to thy good truth and honour.'

It's all a bit bemusing for us as audience. Was this a test of Macduff's integrity and worthiness – that he would not stand in the support of 'evil'? Did Macduff have to pass this test before having the Grail handed to him to do what must be done?

Following this scene, it then naturally fell to Malcolm to fell the trees of Birnam Wood to be borne to Dunsinane in order to surprise the over-confident tyrant.

'Let every soldier hew him down a bough, and bear't before him, thereby shall we shadow the numbers of our host, and make discovery err in report of us.' – Macbeth, Act 5, Scene 4.

In his inimitable way, Shakespeare herewith grants the staff of power to *'every soldier'*, every spiritual warrior who takes responsibility for his own burden in his way is part of the defeat of, *'the confident tyrant who keeps still in Dunsinane, and will endure our setting down before't.'*

The Bearing of the Cross from Jerusalem to Calvary

If we look at the spiritual symbolism in the iconic scene where Jesus bears the cross on his back from Jerusalem to Calvary we can see how it had to be Malcolm's turn to step into the Christ role.

Jerusalem was the Royal City. It is the city of David and Solomon, Kings of the Jews in both the physical and spiritual sense. Jerusalem means 'city of peace'. It symbolises the very heart of the Promised Land, the Kingdom of God.

Calvary was a hill outside the city walls. It symbolises the false world of Satan that has no place in the true kingdom of the divine.

Ironically, the cross symbolises the 'crossing out' of Satan. Jesus did not die on the cross – but Satan did. I'm not saying Jesus 'survived the crucifixion' in the secular, Da Vinci Code sense, but in order for him to triumph over the tyranny of 'good and evil', his body needed to die. The New Testament had to be sealed in his blood. The Old Testament, the sin of the world, could only be fulfilled in a very specific way and this action was an intrinsic element. Portia in the next chapter gives us more insight into the implications of this action.

On the cross, according to the Gospels, the body of Jesus the man, died. But Jesus the Christ demonstrated the ultimate possibility of the soul – a muse of fire that would ascend the brightest heaven of invention.

The Final Showdown – The Virgin Birth

The final showdown is a duel between Macbeth and Macduff. Macbeth in himself is certain of victory. He taunts Macduff about the witches' prophesy, that none of woman born can harm him. Then Macduff delivers the bad news, the ironic twist that he was not of woman born, because from his mother's womb he was – 'untimely ripp'd'.

'Despair thy charm, and let the Angel whom thou still has serv'd tell thee, Macduff was from his mother's womb untimely ripp'd.' – Macbeth, Act 5, Scene 8.

If Shakespeare had wanted to keep these Christ motifs as cryptic as they are, he could hardly have said Macduff's mother had been a virgin! But the implication is nevertheless very clear – there was something very special about the birth of the one who vanquished the tyrant.

Orson Welles disappoints just a tad in his version by changing the word 'Angel' in the text to 'Devil' – it seems to make more sense? But is this the clinching allusion? It could be an allusion to the fallen angel, Satan or I prefer to think it's the Angel Gabriel alluded to here? The Archangel who gave Mary the news of her divine pregnancy?

Shaken but undeterred, Macbeth famously cries '*lay on Macduff, and damned be him , that first cries hold, enough.*'

After a mighty struggle (offstage) Macbeth is defeated. Many directors play this scene *on stage* for cathartic effect – but, as if there weren't enough motifs already, this misses the rather significant one of 'the harrowing of hell' where Jesus is said to have descended into hell to free the souls in bondage. Macduff's return with Macbeth's severed head is an important icon reprising David's beheading the fallen Goliath, another symbol of Satan (Serpent) decapitated.

No sooner is the 'spiritual warrior' role complete than Macduff hands the Grail, the staff of power to Malcolm, the rightful heir to the 'golden round'.

The Comforter

Earlier, Ross, true to his character as narrator, brought in yet another motif, the comforter of Pentecost. He helps us understand why Macduff (another in the line of spiritual kings) has deserted his family in their darkest hour. Can you sense the same feelings of abandonment in Lady Macduff as the disciples of Jesus probably had at his ascension?

117

'*You know not whether it was his wisdom or his fear,*' Ross says to Lady Macduff. — *Macbeth*, Act 4, Scene 2.

'*Wisdom!*' she replies, '*To leave his wife, to leave his babes, his mansion and his titles in a place from whence himself does fly? He loves us not; he wants the natural touch: for the poor wren, the most diminutive of birds, will fight, her young ones in her nest, against the owl. All is the fear and nothing is the love; as little is the wisdom, where the flight so runs against all reason.*'

'*My dearest coz, I pray you, school yourself: but for your husband, he is noble, wise, judicious, and best knows the fits o' the season. I dare not speak much further; but cruel are the times, when we are traitors and do not know ourselves, when we hold rumour from what we fear, yet know not what we fear, but float upon a wild and violent sea each way and move.*'

Lady Macduff mirrors so closely how the disciples must have felt before the coming of the comforter of Pentecost. The comfort of the Grail within? The comfort of *The Tempest* — a wild and violent sea.

And, as he always does to validate our hypothesis, Shakespeare naturally enough employs Macduff to bring *comfort* to the armies of the King — by way of Macbeth's severed head, signifying the end of Satan's rule!

'*Here comes newer comfort.*' — Siward 5:7

Forgiveness of Sin

One of the great misunderstandings keeping us trapped in the bondage and karma of inescapable guilt is that '*we are all sinners and need to beg God to forgive us*'. According to the Gospel, as he died on the cross, Jesus said, '*Father, forgive them; for they know not what they do.*' — Luke 23:34. It's easy to assume this only applied to his killers. And in order to get God's forgiveness we need the agency of a priest. But it is an empirical, psycho-spiritual Truth (meaning we can check this out directly) that we do not get free from guilt or resentment until we resolve it within ourselves.

God is within. God is who we really are, the soul. Neither the greater God of which we are an inseparable part, nor the individualised soul needs to forgive us or anyone — as Portia tells us in Part 2, the attribute of God is not revenge but mercy — because God makes no judgment of us in the first place. The false god does judge us — all the time — that's the point!

If the priest facilitates our self-forgiveness then it works. But if we have to minister to ourselves anyway, why create a dependency on an external agency?

If you're in the business of profiting from selling God's forgiveness or keeping us under control through guilt, then this is not good news.

In a theologically crucial scene that, unlike many directors, Welles did not omit, Shakespeare slips this gem in quietly under the radar.

Lady Macbeth, as the apotheosis of the Abel archetype, is dying of guilt and regret. Macbeth visits her and asks the doctor (priest) if there is a cure for her guilt,

'Canst Thou not minister to a mind diseased, pluck from the memory a rooted sorrow, raze out the written troubles of the brain, and with some sweet oblivious antidote cleanse the stuff'd bosom, of that perilous stuff which weighs upon the heart?' — Macbeth, Act 5, Scene 3.

The doctor replies, *'Therein the patient must minister to himself.' — Macbeth*, Act 5, Scene 4.

The Rialto Bridge

Thus on this note of self-forgiveness for the seemingly unforgiveable, *Macbeth* makes the perfect Rialto Bridge to take us from the Old to the New Testaments where in the platinum haze of Venice's waters, Portia has something vital to say on the sanctity of our word, grace, rude will, and the quality of mercy.

The revelation from *Macbeth* is how critical were the ingredients in the recipe that enabled the law (of Moses) not to be destroyed or dishonoured but fulfilled. There's an exactness in the law that has to be balanced. The way things were, mankind had no choice other than a law that was (and still is) impossible to balance. Through the 'cutting off the head' of Satan (Macbeth), the absolute rule by the mind over the spirit was ended. With Malcolm's (The soul's) rule restored, we have a new choice available: to forgive — but, as Shylock shows with dire consequence, a choice there is no compulsion to make.

PART 2
SHAKESPEARE'S GOSPEL

CHAPTER FOUR
The Merchant of Venice

Shylock's Choice

'And if it seem evil unto you to serve the Lord, choose you this day whom ye will serve . . . but as for me and my house, we will serve the Lord.' – Joshua 24:15

All along, Shakespeare is telling us that before we brush our teeth, drink our coffee, and eat our toast, we have one simple, fundamental choice to make every single day. All choices have consequences – not choosing is also a choice. Unlike worldly choices where there is sensory evidence and emotional compulsion, there is a higher choice that is both positive and neutral. All he or any master can do is bring it to our attention. When we are aware and when we are ready, it will be waiting.

Portia echoes Macbeth by underlining how the law of Moses was never intended to be kept, but intended to keep us in bondage to guilt. The exactness the law demands makes it impossible to keep – even with the most determined and faithful observance. The more diligently we try, the more unworthy we get to feel. The more we seek justice and vengeance from our all-too-human perspective, the more embroiled in endless cycles of karma and payback we become.

Thanks to the Christ action, we all have the choice available to forgive ourselves for the spiritual crime of self-judgment – where we have usurped God in our consciousness and made judgment in His stead. The inconvenient truth is: individual and world peace is totally dependent on this one choice that, in the mind, is the toughest of all to make.

The much misunderstood *Merchant of Venice* is still my favourite play. Not only is it a feast of mystical poetry, an exposition of Shakespeare's spiritual psychology, and a priceless lesson in soul-centred living, but also another nail in the coffin of the religious dogma that keeps mankind as trapped by illusion as it was in 6,000 BCE. A nail that pierces the hand of God and tells us how and why we can step free. A nail that tells us what really happened on Good Friday, 33 CE.

The journal work here is quite tough. Bring to mind agreements you have made and broken. They do not need to be major ones – like fidelity in marriage – it's the little insignificant-seeming ones that whittle away our self-confidence. Paying attention to and learning to honour our word is axiomatic to soul-centred coaching. The question is: what do you make more important than your word? (Hint: others' approval and avoidance of conflict are in the top ten).

When our gondola arrives in Elsinore, Shakespeare expresses this choice through *Hamlet* as '*To be, or not to be?*' In Verona, Friar Laurence gave us 'Grace or Rude Will'? Earlier in Venice, Bassanio had to choose between two gilded impostors and a humble Truth that gave him entry to heaven. Again in Venice Othello had two voices to choose from. Here, now, as we return once more to Venice it is Shylock who is asked to choose 'Revenge or Mercy'? All choice has consequences. Shylock's has the toughest and the direst.

Satan's PR

Satan's cunning PR machine has won him a reputation as being the bad-ass of the universe, the apotheosis of evil. In the mind, it looks like we have a simple choice between the opposites of good and evil. If I choose good, it means I'm not

THE MERCHANT OF VENICE
THE WORD MADE FLESH

"Come ho, and wake Diana with a hymn! With sweetest touches pierce your mistress' ear and draw her home with music."

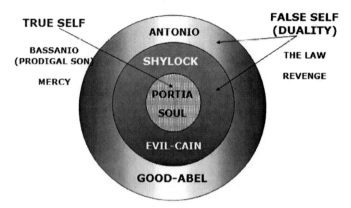

choosing evil. In religious terms, choosing to be good means I'm not choosing Satan, therefore choosing God.

But what if Satan is both? What if good and evil are not opposites, but the same substance fiendishly cast in opposition so we are sucked into never-ending dilemma?

As Shakespeare's archetypes, good and evil are cast in the same metal, the same coin: Goneril and Regan. Gold and silver. Othello and Iago. Antonio and Shylock.

Is silver the opposite of gold? When neither gets you into Belmont. Choosing good over evil is not the way to heaven!

Is rabbit the opposite of duck? Is good the opposite of bad? Right the opposite of wrong? Right the opposite of left?

When we choose to be good in any way that implies an opposition, a judgment that we are better or more righteous than any other person we are playing Satan's right hand against his left. And all we hear is the hollow applause of self-congratulation. If all we see is 'good and evil' it makes little difference

123

which we choose. To make a difference, we need to choose the seagull, the higher, transcendent, invisible, inner choice neither duck nor rabbit, neither good nor evil.

Gospel: Good News or Bad?

'Gospel' means 'good news'. But over the centuries, the belief that the way to be 'saved' is to choose a very specific way of being good, meant 'bad news' for a lot of people. Very bad news. And continues to this day so to do.

'In the beginning was the Word.' – John 1:1.

'And the Word was made flesh, and dwelt among us.' – John 1:14.

If you were Shakespeare looking for a way to tell mankind what the good news in the Gospel really is, would you pick these two enigmatic lines? Frankly, would you even know what they really mean?

Let's add in this verse and see what happens:

'Greater love hath no man than this, that a man lay down his life for his friends.' – John 15:13.

Now we have something. Could this be the basis of an intensely dramatic fusion of biblical allegories centred about Antonio, a wealthy, righteous, Christian merchant who's got all his money tied up in some precious cargoes at the mercy of the tempests at sea? He has a strange sadness overshadowing him that he knows not from whence it comes. Perhaps a nagging foreboding that something awful will befall him? Perhaps Shakespeare's way of dramatising one of the key learnings from the play – the price we pay when we do not honour our word and treat it with disdain. Giving our word away casually to gain approval and breaking it with an apology later is a pandemic human pattern, that automatically cuts us off from the divine energy from the soul. It unconsciously drains our energy and, as we'll see, puts all our relationships in jeopardy. In Antonio's case something close to his heart is about to be cut off – quite literally. Shakespeare goes a very long way to make a very small point – a point as sharp as a hypodermic needle injecting a powerful Truth into our bloodstream.

His friend, Gratiano observes, '*You look not well, Signor Antonio. You have too much respect upon the world.*' Antonio replies, '*I hold the world but as the world, Gratiano – A stage where every man must play a part, and mine a sad one*', and immediately confirms our hypothesis establishing Antonio as playing the role of the Abel archetype. He sports the image of a 'good' man, but confesses he cannot see beyond the worldly senses. In other words, he has too much invested in the world and not enough in his own spiritual self.

Which is why he is not predisposed to looking within himself for higher spiritual guidance. Foolish man. Will your sandy foundations stand when the winds and rains beat upon your house?

Antonio's dearest, closest friend, young Lord Bassanio, desperately needs three thousand ducats so he can woo the beautiful, wealthy Portia, hazard all he has to win her hand, and unburden himself from all the debts he has.

Antonio so loves Bassanio, a self-confessed prodigal, like his only begotten son. So great is his love that to help his friend, he agrees to borrow the money in the certain knowledge that his ships will soon be home with his fortune. He commits himself to borrowing three thousand ducats for three months from a scurrilous Jew named Shylock. A Jew upon whom he spits for no other reason that he is what he is – a Jew.

Shylock is a notoriously successful usurer. He also has cause to despise Antonio probably even more than the anti-Semitic, bigoted Antonio has to despise him. Shylock, sensing an opportunity to use the law to avenge the years of disrespect, degradation, and phlegm, he has borne at the wrong end of Antonio's mouth, agrees to the loan – on one condition: that if Antonio defaults on the repayment, he, Shylock, is entitled by legally binding bond to carve a pound of flesh from any part of Antonio's body he so desires.

This is the Cain archetype, like Iago, feeling the affront, the profound disrespect for the essence of who he is (a soulless vessel), seeking the death of his brother.

Shylock cares nothing for this money – he has a cache of gold in his house. Shylock wants revenge. Antonio seems prepared to lay down his life for his friend. He has blind faith in the certain return of his ships with his merchandise within two months – a full month before the cut-off date. His pound of flesh is surely safe … so he gives his word to Shylock and thereby enters a legally binding contract.

Antonio's word is now made flesh.

And Great was His Fall

What befalls Antonio is inevitable – it would have been a dull play had it not. He falls headlong into Shylock's trap. The 'tempest' shakes the sandy foundations upon which he has built his castle. All his ships founder at sea. He cannot repay the loan. He defaults on his agreement. He is now bound by his word to give Shylock his pound of flesh. Already a wealthy man, Shylock cares nothing for the money. He wants his revenge. His bond. His bond is his by law. He will not be swayed otherwise. He wants his pound of flesh. He deserves his pound of flesh. He is entitled to his pound of flesh.

End of.

True to archetype, his *'perfect reasons'* are, well, perfect.

'If you prick us, do we not bleed? If you tickle us, do we not laugh? If you poison us, do we not die? And if you wrong us, shall we not revenge? If we are like you in the rest, we will resemble you in that. If a Jew wrong a Christian, what is his humility? Revenge. If a Christian wrong a Jew, what should his sufferance be by Christian example? Why, revenge. The villainy you teach me, I will execute, and it shall go hard but I Will better the instruction.' – Shylock, *The Merchant of Venice*, Act 3, Scene I.

Shylock will give no quarter. The case now goes to trial. Antonio is doomed.

Bassanio, the prodigal son, returns to Venice – now a rich, married man. Adam is reunited with his Eve. He offers Shylock twice, thrice, ten times the sum to show mercy to his friend. But no. Shylock wants what is his right by law.

The same way we saw Iago and Othello as two sides of the same coin, so are Antonio and Shylock. The equivalent false selves in us feel divided, conflicted sympathies. With whom do you sympathise? Do you want Shylock to have his vengeance? Should he be given what is his right by law? Should Antonio be smitten for being an anti-Semite? Or should he be shown mercy because he's such a great friend and all-round nice guy?

Man's Dilemma and the Law

This is the dilemma of man, in black-and-white. Both sides are right. Both sides are also wrong. This is the game of life where nobody wins.

Enter another verse from John, 1:17: *'For the law was given by Moses, but grace and truth came by Jesus Christ.'*

Enter Portia, cross-dressed as a young man, a doctor of law, with the Wisdom of Solomon in her heart.

As the soul, she is not here to judge but to soar above the dilemma like a seagull and see things just as they are.

She hears the pleas on both sides and decides, *'The Jew must be merciful'*. Quite in archetype, the Jew retorts, *'On what compulsion, must I? Tell me that.'* – The Merchant of Venice, Act 4, Scene I.

And tell him she does: she offers him a choice – to choose the Law of Moses, the law of an eye-for-an-eye, the law of 'good and evil', the law of rude will, the law given by the impostor, the law of Satan, the law of karma that keeps us all in bondage – or to choose mercy, and forgiveness, the grace of God, through the Christ, the soul within us all. How do we know this? In one of his most spiritually moving speeches, Portia tells us,

'The quality of mercy is not strain'd, It droppeth as the gentle rain from heaven upon the place beneath. It is twice blest: It blesseth him that gives and him that takes ... it is an attribute to God himself: and earthly power doth then show likest God's when mercy seasons justice ... ' – The Merchant of Venice, Act 4, Scene I.

Shylock, however, is not moved. He demands the law. He wants revenge. He wants justice.

Portia warns him, *'That in the course of justice none of us should see salvation.'*

But the Cain-self, Shylock, is lost to his soul, suffering from terminal lack of respect, seeks to kill his brother hoping to kill the pain of his alienation, *'My deeds upon my head! I crave the law, the penalty and forfeit of my bond.'*

What befalls Shylock is inevitable – it would have been a dull play had it not. He chooses the law. He demands his bond. He demands his right to his bond and his right to the judgment of law. And as he strops his razor to carve his pound of flesh, Portia halts him and begs him consider the true nature of justice, *'For, as thou urgest justice, be assur'd thou shalt have justice, more than thou desir'st.'*

But again, he is unmoved. So now, having committed himself to the law, there is no turning back. He will have his law — and everything that goes with it.

He is now required by that same law to exact said pound of flesh. That's exactly one pound, no more, no less … and on pain of forfeiture of all his goods and land, may not one drop of blood be spilled. Isn't it interesting, so many of the plays end in a blood bath. In this, where everything hangs on one drop of blood, not one drop is spilled.

'Tarry a little. There is something else. This bond doth give thee here no jot of blood. The words expressly are 'a pound of flesh.'Take then thy bond, take thou thy pound of flesh, but in the cutting it if thou dost shed one drop of Christian blood, thy lands and goods are by the laws of Venice confiscate unto the state of Venice.' — Portia, *The Merchant of Venice* Act 4, Scene I.

Realising he is hoist by his own petard, Shylock now tries to wriggle off the hook. He agrees to take the earlier offer of thrice times the bond. But it's too late. He has committed himself to choosing the law. And all choices have consequences.

Enter another verse, this time from Matthew 5:18 *'For verily I say unto you, till heaven and earth pass, one jot or one tittle shall in no wise pass from the law, till all be fulfilled.'* (Jot and tittle are the smallest possible things one can imagine.)

The same spiritual principle in Portia's solemn words, sounds like, *'Therefore prepare thee to cut off the flesh. Shed thou no blood, nor cut thou less nor more than a just pound — be it so much as makes it light or heavy in the substance, or the division of the twentieth part of one poor scruple; nay, if the scale do turn but in the estimation of a hair [shy of a lock!] — thou diest, and all thy goods are confiscate.'The Merchant of Venice*, Act 4, Scene I.

One again the symbolism of the original Eucharist is right here. Body and blood. Bread and wine. Sound and light. They are one in us as we are one in God. To know God in our own heart we need them both. To separate the two is (biblical) death – banishment. And this is what Shylock as Cain brought upon himself – banishment.

Shylock knows he's lost everything, his revenge and his bond are gone. He tries to exit the court. But Portia stops him and informs him the law (that he so craved) is now going to take another bite out of his flesh. He's now found guilty of attempted murder and thus according to the law of Venice he insisted upon using, half his estate goes to Antonio, the other half to the state, and his very life rests upon the mercy of the presiding Duke. The Duke immediately shows mercy but he's left penniless. His daughter has also eloped taking all his hoard of gold. He has nothing left for his pains – nothing except his precious law, his insatiable craving for revenge and justice, and, oh yes – his new religion.

Good Christian Antonio gives Shylock yet another choice. To keep his half of his wealth if he bequeaths it to his (despised) son-in-law and becomes a Christian. Is this as payback, a sincere regard that Shylock's soul be saved, or just the arrogant, demi-god archetype making itself seem all-powerful? That's up to us to decide. I know which way I jump. Has the Antonio in us learnt its lesson, or has it been let off the hook only to wriggle its way into making more trouble for the burgeoning soul?

Are we now feeling sorry for Shylock? We hated him a few minutes ago for his stubborn cruelty, and now he's so hard done by, it's not fair.

Whose Trial is it Anyway?

It's no surprise this trial has an ironic twist. Shylock indicts Antonio and is himself indicted by the very law he is using against him.

However, given what *Macbeth* taught us about Shakespeare's Modus Operandi with Christ Motifs, is there yet another twist in the tale? Whose trial do you think this symbolises? Whose body and blood?

An outraged Jew (Shylock) demands the death of a Christian and takes him before the court of Venice. Seventeen hundred years earlier, an outraged Jew (Caiaphas) demands the death of a Christ and takes him before the court of Rome!

'Then Pilate entered into the judgment hall again, and called Jesus, and said unto him, art thou the King of the Jews? Jesus answered him, Sayest thou this thing of thyself, or did others tell it thee of me? Pilate answered, Am I a Jew? Thine own nation and the chief priests have delivered thee unto me: what hast thou done? Jesus answered, My kingdom is not of this world: if my kingdom were of this world, then would my servants fight, that I should not be delivered to the Jews: but now is my kingdom not from hence. Pilate therefore said unto him, Art thou a king then? Jesus answered, Thou sayest that I am a king. To this end was I born, and for this cause came I into the world, that I should bear witness unto the truth. Every one that is of the truth heareth my voice. Pilate saith unto him, What is truth? And when he had said this, he went out again unto the Jews, and saith unto them, I find in him no fault at all. But ye have a custom, that I should release unto you one at the Passover: will ye therefore that I release unto you the King of the Jews? Then cried they all again, saying, Not this man, but Barabbas. Now Barabbas was a robber.' – John 18, 33–40.

Who really died on the cross?

When they put the crown of thorns (the hollow crown) on Jesus' head, the label 'INRI', and crucified him, they thought they were killing the Christ. But they did not succeed. It was only an *attempt* to kill the Christ that failed. How do we know? The Christ rose from the dead and dwelt among them. *In the Spirit on the Lord's Day*, the seven seals were opened. The sound of the waters could once again be heard and the soul was now free to leave this world and return home to God.

As a delicious parallel with the irony in the trial of Antonio by Shylock, simply the *attempt* by the Sanhedrin to kill the Christ brought the law down upon their heads. The irony of the crucifixion is that Christ resurrected and Satan was deposed. The death and resurrection of Christ was the last prophesy that had to be fulfilled in order for the law of Moses to be completed and the New Testament to be initiated.

The allusion in Shylock's trial (a pound of flesh – but not one jot of blood) was to the body and the blood being as one. This is a further motif of the last supper where it is the re-union of the body and blood (the sound and the light) that makes the once-lost holy communion possible again. Possible through asking for the light and calling the Name of God in unison (bread and wine) – as it was in the beginning when the Word was made flesh.

This means we have two new choices: we can now choose grace, mercy, and forgiveness to enjoy on this level, and we can also choose to transcend the consciousness of 'good and evil' and live in the consciousness of soul. This is how Revelation says the New Jerusalem, the new state of consciousness was established and made available as a choice,

'And I saw a new heaven and a new earth: for the first heaven and the first earth were passed away; and there was no more sea. And I John saw the holy city, New Jerusalem, coming down from God out of heaven, prepared as a bride adorned for her husband. And I heard a great voice out of heaven saying, Behold, the tabernacle of God is with men, and he will dwell with them, and they shall be his people, and God himself shall be with them, and be their God. And God shall wipe away all tears from their eyes; and there shall be no more death, neither sorrow, nor crying, neither shall there be any more pain: for the former things are passed away.' – Revelation 21, 1–4.

Portia's Portion

Here's the reveal of the likely true, inner meaning of the name 'P O R T I A'. If we temper the law with mercy, forgiveness, and compassion, the deeper teaching of the Christ says all we are required to do in order to balance our (karmic) debt is our 'P O R T I O N'. The gap between what is needed so exactly to balance the law that it is impossible for any human to repay, and the *portion* of this we are capable of doing is *fulfilled* through grace. If we do not choose grace, if we insist on the law, if we demand vengeance, strive to get even in our own way, we're on our own. We forfeit grace, lose what we have, and accrue endless cycles of karma, debt, and hell on earth.

If we forgive ourselves and our judgments of others, if we do the best we can, if we honour our word as a bond between the conscious self that resides here in the world and the soul deep within, we automatically open the door for spiritual assistance. This is a far cry from being sanctimonious and self-righteous, this is about being non-judgmental, and having personal integrity.

Shylock is my Name

Othello often gets accused of being the racist play, *The Merchant* of being anti-Semitic. As one of life's great mirrors, the plays will reflect back to us whatever we put in front of them. Our interpretations are our own.

Here's another perspective:

At the start of the trial scene, when Portia asks who Shylock, the plaintiff is, she does not turn to him and simply say, 'Are you Shylock?' She specifically asks, '*Is your name Shylock?*' Shylock rather than simply replying 'yes', or 'I am Shylock', replies very pointedly, '*Shylock is my name.*' This makes a very fine, subtle, distinction. It confirms he is not *defining* himself as his name only using the name as a *label for the archetype.*

And – this is critically important – the archetype is independent of race, colour or religion. Shylock is the *characterisation* of the false self that usurps the true self of man. The *archetype* of the *Cain* false self is that part in all of us that cannot forgive, that demands revenge, that craves 'an eye for an eye', that refuses to show mercy, that must have the law. Whenever any of us – whatever religion, philosophy or belief system we subscribe to – lets those primitive, base, feelings of revenge and hatred dictate our behaviour, we are acting the 'Shylock'.

But what could the name Shylock itself mean? It is not a known Jewish (or any racial) name. Is it another of Shakespeare's poignant concoctions?

Here's Shakespeare's awesome irony and wordsmithery coming into play again. The name 'Shylock' seems to contain a double-entendre.

First entendre could be: we know from Cordelia (Coeur de Lear) how Shakespeare loves his homonyms, words that sound like other words but have a different meaning. When I listen to the sound of the name 'Shylock' I hear 'Side-lock'. A side lock is the Anglicisation of the Hebrew word 'Payas', the uncut lock of hair worn at the temple by some observant Jews as a sign of their devotion to the law (of Moses).

In the context we have been exploring, this is where my money goes. On the surface, the name 'Shylock' is a synecdoche for 'Jew'. But the deeper meaning refers to all of us when we crave the law rather than show mercy.

The second entendre could be Shakespeare enjoying a wee pun. For, as we saw, it was down to the minute twentieth part of one poor scruple, *'nay, if the scale do turn but in the estimation of a hair [shy of a lock!] – thou diest, and all thy goods are confiscate.'*, where Shylock's craving for the law came back and ripped the pound of flesh from his own heart.

Bassanio has the Last Word

'Now the serpent was more subtil than any beast of the field which the Lord God had made.' Genesis 3:1.

Lest we forget, let's let Bassanio have the last word. Not only is Shakespeare giving us a mystical, theological, discourse he is also giving us a lesson in practical spirituality. As I have been at pains to learn the priceless value of my word, so is Bassanio. On their marriage, Portia gives him a ring. The ring symbolises her undying love and her giving to him all her wealth. He swears an oath that the only way he will be parted from the ring is if he is dead. *'But when this ring parts from this finger, parts life from hence.'* – The Merchant of Venice, Act 3, Scene 2.

It's an ironic mirror of the bond between Antonio and Shylock.

Now comes the life lesson I have also learnt the hard way. When I make an agreement, when I give my word to another, who am I really making the agreement with? My self. My soul. Whether I like it or not. Whether I know it or not, when I make an agreement, I am bound to it. Shakespeare is making this point very poignantly. Even if I agree to something trivial (like wearing a cheap ring) it's not the action or the object that matters but my *word*.

If I squander my word, I have *no choice* but to forfeit the divine aid from my own soul. If I treasure my word – only give it away when I am willing to honour it – I *automatically* gain the confidence and integrity of my soul within. This is the axiom of modern spiritual psychology dramatised for us in the seventeenth century.

How many times do we give our word away carelessly or even deceitfully? Every time we do this, it's not a moral issue, it's not 'wrong' – it's just very expensive. And the converse is also true. Learning how to work with our inner spirit is fundamental to developing personal integrity and gaining trust, respect and understanding in our relationships.

135

After Portia, still unrecognised, disguised as a man, saves the life of Bassanio's friend Antonio, she tests her husband's honour. She asks for nothing by way of reward save the said ring on Bassanio's finger. It's not our worthiness to enter the Kingdom that is tested, but our readiness. Have we learnt the lessons we came to earth to learn? At first he refuses, playing it down, saying it is a mere trifle, surely she could have something greater? He knows its 'other' value, *'There's more depends on this than on the value, the dearest ring in Venice I will give you.'* — The Merchant of Venice, Act 4, Scene I.

But Portia, who is no dunce with a persuasive word, drives the dagger of *need for approval* into him up to the hilt. He passes this test and still holds true to his word — until Antonio (the false self) steps in and entreats Bassanio to break it! It is Antonio that still totally fails to learn the lesson he has just escaped from with his life. He doesn't value his own word and nearly paid for this with his life, likewise he cannot appreciate the priceless value Bassanio placed in his word. He now puts the emotional pressure of withdrawal of love and guilt on Bassanio. He puts his dearest friend's blessed relationship with Portia in jeopardy. He risks destroying the very thing he was willing to lay down his life for.

'My Lord Bassanio,' begs Antonio, *'let him have the ring. Let his deservings, and my love withal be valued 'gainst your wife's commandment.'* — The Merchant of Venice, Act 4, Scene I.

It all looks so 'reasonable' — after all the 'doctor' did save the day, he is the hero, he should have whatever he wants, surely? This is absolutely the intention of the false self — to undermine the soul in every way. Bassanio feels but cannot quite cognise consequences. He is torn between the loss of Antonio's approval (a symbol of love) and the loss of a ring that symbolises Portia's love. He misses the point that it's not the symbol he's giving away, but the real thing, his word, his bond to his soul. And Bassanio falls. He gives the ring, his word, his soul, his life, away for the mingy reward of 'approval'.

In contrast to Shylock in the same situation, Portia does show mercy. Not before she confronts him with his broken agreement, has him consider the price he has paid, and challenges him to be more aware of the pearl of great price nesting in his mouth. Bassanio's 'portion', is to acknowledge his error and vow not to do the same again. As we are all a god-in-training, this is the best we can ever be expected to do. The whole scene is played in a 'light-hearted' way. And all's well that ends well. But the lesson, the life-changing principle, is nevertheless brought home.

The Four Keys to Keeping Your Word

If you want the automatic rewards of self-confidence and trusting relationships that come from honouring your word and agreements – no matter what:

- Make your agreements important.

- Write them down.

- Only make agreements you intend to keep.

- Renegotiate agreements (whenever possible) rather than just break them with an apology.

Why Venice is Such an Important Setting

Such harmony is in immortal souls, but whilst this muddy vesture of decay doth grossly close it in, we cannot hear it. Come ho, and wake Diana with a hymn! With sweetest touches pierce your mistress' ear, and draw her home with music.' – Lorenzo, *The Merchant of Venice*, Act 5, Scene I.

In order to see how perfectly Venice serves Shakespeare's purpose as a setting, we have to do some spiritual exercises. It takes work, it takes a risk, it takes letting go, but we need to make the giant leap of seeing the line of symbols linking: '*the waters*' of Genesis, '*the Word*' of John's Gospel, the '*wind from heaven*' and '*the voice of many waters'* of Revelation, *'The Tempests'* of Shakespeare, and God's divine instrument of creation oft referred to as *'The Sound Current'*! The Bible mixes its metaphors with impunity, and Shakespeare takes the same poetic license.

As an allegorical story doing its best to communicate that which cannot be comprehended by the mind it goes something like this: Out of the harmony of the Sound of God's Name, all life, all souls and all matter is created. Among many things, this sound was called the 'Holy Grail'. As we've just seen dramatised in *Macbeth*, the Grail was lost by Adam and restored by Jesus the Christ. *Macbeth* doesn't really tell us what this is and what it means to us here and now. Enter *The Merchant of Venice*.

If all of God's souls travelled on the *Sound Current* from Spirit to this material world for an experience – and got trapped here by Satan's trickery, then it follows, like the night, the day that the way out is back up to God on the same vehicle, *The Sound Current*. As we go about our lives *'with too much respect upon the world'* we cannot hear the sweet sound of the soul calling us back home.

'Such harmony is in immortal souls, but whilst this muddy vesture of decay doth grossly close it in, we cannot hear it.' – The Merchant of Venice, Act 5, Scene I.

But since the Grail has been restored, Shakespeare is telling us the good news is we now have this new choice to focus inwardly on the soul, call the Name of God and let it take us back to our true home in the heart of God.

'Come ho, and wake Diana with a hymn! With sweetest touches pierce your mistress' ear, and draw her home with music.'

Re-examining John, *'And the Word [the waters] was made flesh and dwelt among us'*, Venice is the city whose waters dwell amongst its people. The deeper point is that *'the waters'* are freely available to everybody to partake of – Jew, Christian, and Moor alike. All God's children have been chosen – no exceptions. All we have to do is choose back. But if we play the games of Shylock and Antonio (Cain and Abel) we lose. If we follow Bassanio's example and learn from his relationship with Portia (the soul) we enter Belmont, Heaven, and Ananda.

Next Steps

Consider the mighty spiritual teaching in John brought to us by Shakespeare. Contemplate it in the light of what we've been exploring. Can you now begin to see how much personal power we squander when we give our word away for trifles and symbols of love? After all, Neither Antonio nor Bassanio had any need to give their word in the first place. Like we do so often, Bassanio gave his word away to impress his new bride with his undying love. In the same way Prospero 'tested' Ferdinand before giving him Miranda's hand, so does Portia test Bassanio.

'In the beginning was the Word, and the Word was with God, and the Word was God. The same was in the beginning with God. All things were made by him; and without him was not any thing made that was made. In him was life; and the life was the light of men. And the light shineth in darkness; and the darkness comprehended it not.' – John I, I–5.

Ignorance is no excuse for breaking the law. Whether we know it or not, believe it or not, accept it or not, in our mouths, the power of the divine, the spirit within, the soul, the Sound, The Name, has been liberated within our consciousness. Now we are free to command and create our own world, our own universe.

What are we going to do with such power? How are we going to vanquish the 'hollow crown' and claim the fullness of our spiritual majesty?

Let's ask Henry V. Let's see in greater detail, how to vanquish Satan and reclaim the Grail within.

CHAPTER FIVE

Henry V

Awaken the Spiritual Warrior within

'If his spirit is distorted he should simply fix it — purge it, make it perfect — because there is no other task in our entire lives which is more worthwhile ... To seek the perfection of the warrior's spirit is the only task worthy of our temporariness, our manhood.' — Carlos Castaneda, *Journey to Ixtlan.*

To find an example of outstanding, authentic leadership we need look no further than *Henry V*. About this, much has already been said and written. What I'd like to do is, once again, look beneath the surface at the deeper spiritual guidance Shakespeare is simultaneously offering us.

Journal work here is to claim the majesty of your own inner world. If you had no fears, no self-doubts, no self-inflicted limitations, what goals would you set yourself. What do you really want to do and be?

Through the four plays, *Richard II, Henry IV Parts 1 and 2,* and *Henry V,* rather than create fictional characters like Othello, Shakespeare casts personages from history in his allegory of the soul's evolutionary journey from Eden to hell-on-earth and back again. In so doing, he is delineating the steps in a route map of how we can once more take charge of our own destiny, rout the impostors who usurp our lives from within, and rise to the highest pinnacles of possibility.

'O for a muse of fire, that would ascend the brightest heaven of invention.' — Prologue, *Henry V.*

With this prayer, Shakespeare calls upon us to follow in the footsteps of Henry V as the fire of his soul is ignited and he extinguishes all tyrannies that stand in his way.

The story of the vanquishing of Macbeth (Satan) by the line of kings (Banquo–Macduff–Malcolm) and the restoration of the Grail, is the self-same story as the rise of Henry V in restoring the rightful crown to 'the world's best garden' (France) – and the self-same keys to how we can restore the soul that we really are back to the centre of consciousness where it truly belongs.

'Christ Motifs' jaunce through the *Henriad* as in *Macbeth*. I've pounced on some, but I dearly recommend you re-visit the play and see what others pop up for you. I assume Shakespeare's alchemy will enable us to see the ones we're ready to see – and remain oblivious to those we are not.

The Spiritual Warrior

John-Roger, in his book, *Spiritual Warrior*, talks of the *'intention, impeccability and ruthlessness'* required to live an inner spiritual life in a constantly changing, and demanding world. Great sages often speak of detachment and overcoming desire as major keys. None of this is particularly easy – nor is a life spent chasing worthless symbols of success and importance.

'Intention is the direction we want to take. Spiritual Warriors make sure their intention is very clear because what we put out into the world is what we get back. If your intention is to be loving and caring, you cannot let anything that is not loving or caring come into your field of action.

'Impeccability is, quite simply, using our energy wisely and purposefully, conserving and directing it so that we align ourselves with Spirit. From this spiritual alignment emerges clarity about eternal reality and freedom from the binding nature of the physical world.

'Ruthlessness is the Spiritual Warrior's Sword of Truth, the Sword of the Heart, which cuts away all that is no longer necessary or useful. Spiritual Warriors do not accept just anything and everything but are ruthless about ridding themselves of limitations and addictions – the habitual unproductive behaviours of the past.' – John-Roger, *Spiritual Warrior*.

This is exactly what we see Harry doing. The entire 'Henriad' is predicated on demonstrating these universal principles.

As I look into my own life, I see how attached I am to many things *that don't look like symbols at all*. My wife, *my* horses, *my* house, and *my* work, the work I have created from nothing out of a single idea. Nota Bene: the possessive pronoun. This view of *my* 'things' binds me to them. The thought of letting them go, living my life without them is an unbearable nightmare. Divorce my wife. Give my horses away. Stop riding. Stop working. Aaaaaaaaargh!

But this is not true detachment. True detachment is enjoying everything I have in the deeper knowing that if the worst came to worst and I did lose everything (as did Lear) then I'm still ok. I'll find a way through. I don't have to hang on to 'things' for my security. That's not building on rock. Rock is the soul, my true self. That's who I am. That's 'all' I have. That's everything that, as Hamlet reflects on, in the shadow of the mind, seems somewhere between a dilemma and the void of death.

Yes, banish the false self, and banish the world, the false world of lies and illusions. Welcome the real world, the world of truth, joy, and abundant prosperity.

Begin With the End in Mind

The eulogy at the end of Henry's fast-burning life reminds us who he symbolised, and what he achieved:

'*This star of England. Fortune made his sword; by which the world's best garden he achieved.*' – *Henry V*, Act 5, Scene 2.

If *Richard II* symbolises the fall of Adam and, with it, the fall of man's soul into Satan's trap, then *Henry V* symbolises how he used '*the sword of truth*' to resurrect

Richard and vanquish Satan. It's the same story we saw in *Macbeth* and *Othello* acted out from a different angle and with greater elaboration of the details of the process of reclaiming our spiritual Truth.

'Thou, old Adam's likeness, set to dress this garden how dares thy harsh tongue sound this unpleasing news? What Eve, what serpent, hath suggested thee to make a second fall of cursed man?' – Queen, *Richard II*, Act 3, Scene 4.

I must be on my guard not to be seduced by the glamour of the characterisations, but stay vigilant to the quest of seeing them all as our multi-dimensional, inner states of consciousness. Our focus here is on how Shakespeare is delineating the process and the key steps we must take if we are to do battle with the negative forces within us and climb Jacob's Ladder all the way back home.

One key step well-documented in most spiritual teachings is 'initiation'. Before we consider Hal's initiation and what this means for us, let's get to grips with some of the archetypes.

The Archetypes: *Henry IV, Part 1*

After Bolingbroke deposes Richard II to become Henry IV, we rejoin him in England to begin the (outer) story of how his son Hal, Prince of Wales, earns his right of passage to the throne and the title King Henry V. Don't enjoy it too much least you forget this is the inner *you* Shakespeare is depicting!

From the start, Hal certainly has his work cut out.

At the beginning of the story, Hal, like Bassanio, is the one cast as *'the prodigal son'*. As such, he is an outsider, banished from the orbit of the soul still occupied by the invisible 'ghost' of Richard II. The ghost who haunts his unforgiven usurper and refuses to let him sleep.

HENRY V

"O for a muse of fire, that would ascend the brightest heaven of invention."

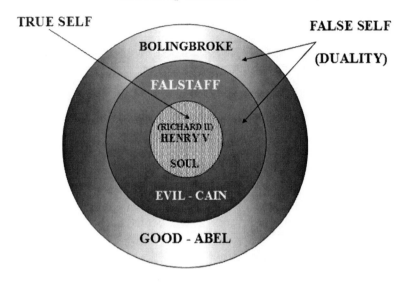

Not that Hal is inclined initially to return home, but standing in his way is his shadow-self, Harry 'Hotspur' Percy. Hotspur not only has the same name and similar age to Hal – he has also usurped his place in his father's heart. Bolingbroke laments that perhaps Hal and Hotspur had been swapped at birth and Percy was his true son!

'Yea, thou there makest me sad, and makest me sin in envy that my Lord Northumberland should be father to so blest a son: a son who is the theme of honour's tongue, amongst a grove the very straightest plant, who is sweet fortune's minion and her pride – whilst I by looking on the praise of him see riot and dishonour stain the brow of my young Harry. O that it could be proved that some night-tripping fairy had exchanged in cradle-clothes our children where they lay, and called mine Percy, his Plantagenet!' – Henry IV pt. I, Act I, Scene I.

Nice thing indeed for a father to say. Especially as his judgment is seriously impaired (no doubt by too much guilt and not enough sleep). We've just heard how he views Hotspur, let's eavesdrop on Hotspur's opinion of Bolingbroke – and Hal:

'... *where I first bowed my knee unto this king of smiles, this Bolingbroke ... why, what a candy deal of courtesy this fawning greyhound then did proffer me!* '*Look when his infant fortune came to age*', *and* '*gentle Harry Percy*', *and* '*kind cousin*'. *O, the devil take such cozeners – God forgive me!*'

'*All studies here I solemnly defy, save how to gall and pinch this Bolingbroke. And that same sword-and-buckler Prince of Wales – but that I think his father loves him not and would be glad he met with some mischance – I would have him poisoned with a pot of ale.*' – Henry IV pt. I, Act I, Scene 3.

As a character, Hotspur's role is multi-faceted. In his desire to kill Hal and usurp the throne, is he the Cain to Bolingbroke's Abel?

Initiation

'*To be an initiate is to devote yourself to the God within you, to Spirit and to returning to your home, the Soul realm, from which you originally came before you incarnated onto this earth.*' – John-Roger, *Fulfilling Your Spiritual Promise*.

Another word for 'rite of passage' is initiation. We can be initiated into all manner of outer things from clubs, secret societies, fraternities, etc. to sacred and secret inner spiritual things. In the realms of spirit, so I am told, there are thousands of light and mystery school initiations occurring all the time as, way beyond our conscious awareness, we are moving on our inner mystical travels.

The initiation that concerns us here, as committed Spiritual Warriors, is known as a Sound Current Initiation. A Sound Current Initiation is the sacred inner-connection of our soul to the current of energy that flows upwards from this physical created world to the realms of the soul and above into God. While available to all who ask and who are ready and willing to undergo considerable testing, Sound Current Initiation itself can only be given by a master who holds the keys to the Sound Current. In the Grail mythology, this personage was called *The*

Fisher King. In the Gospel, the Apostles were probably given this key as Jesus said, *'Follow me, and I will make you fishers of men.'* – Matthew 4:19.

In biblical symbolism, what passes between the master and the neophyte is oft referred to as the Word, the waters, the *stone*, or *True Name* of God.

What we see through Shakespeare's genius in *Henry V* is a man who transforms from a prodigal son with a false name into a true son of the king who unfailingly puts God's True Name before him in all he does.

Hotspur and the Grail

'In thy faint slumbers I by thee have watched, and heard thee murmur tales of iron wars … of prisoners' ransom and of soldiers slain, and all the currents of a heady fight. Thy spirit within thee hath been so at war, and thus has so bestirred thee in thy sleep, that beads of sweat have stood upon thy brow, like bubbles in a late-disturbed stream.' – Lady Percy, Henry IV pt.I, Act 2, Scene 3.

Unwittingly, Hotspur acts as the spark that makes *hot* the *fire* of Hal's Spiritual Warrior and *spurs* him to victory. In *Macbeth*, we see how the Grail is held by the tyrant until reclaimed by the Christ who vanquishes him. In *Henry IV,* Hotspur's wife, in commenting on his fitful sleep, with gossamer subtlety, alludes to the presence of the Sound Current (a late-disturbed stream) flowing within her husband.

When Hal finally slays Hotspur in battle, in sharp contrast to Falstaff's disdain of honour, Hal honours Hotspur as one of Great Spirit within. Before they fight, when Price Harry (no longer 'Hal') remarks that *'Two stars keep not their motion in one sphere'*, Shakespeare is whispering imperceptibly back to allude to a verse in Genesis I, where, before he was betrayed, God (Day) grants Satan (Night) the first covenant. (No, these lights are not 'the sun and the moon'!): *'And God made two great lights; the greater light to rule the day, and the lesser light to rule the night.'* – Genesis I:16.

Symbolically, Hal and Hotspur are fighting over the Grail – the right to rule our inner kingdom. Hotspur falls and in his dying speech says *'But thoughts, the slaves of life, and life, time's fool, and time, that takes survey of all the world, must have a stop.'* – Henry IV pt. I, Act 5, Scene 4.

Henry, in a generous act of forgiveness congruent with his enlightened nature, pays homage to Hotspur's great heart, *'When that his body did contain a spirit, a kingdom for it was too small a bound; but now two paces of the vilest earth is room enough.'*

A Sidebar: Self-Awareness, Horses and Kingdoms

Curiously, Hotspur is also a link in the (unlikely yet quite evident once you expose it) chain of symbolism between the Barbary roan horses of Richard II and Richard III!

What must surely be the obscurest connection in Shakespeare can be made perhaps through the common 'Cain' archetypes. Bolingbroke, Hotspur, and Richard III all play a version of Cain. Could it be that the release of the notorious thief Barabbas in Jesus' stead symbolises how Cain was not killed but sent to walk the earth in some kind of perpetual living perdition?

Compare this from Richard II's final speech, *'I was not made a horse; and yet I bear a burden like an ass, spurr'd, gall'd and tir'd, by jauncing Bolingbroke.'*, with these from Hotspur, *' All studies here I solemnly defy, save how to gall and pinch this Bolingbroke.'*

'Gall and pinch' are an equestrian metaphor for deposing a king. They refer to a girth strap (hollow crown?) that's so tight and ill-fitting for the horse that it causes girth galls – open sores that can fester and cause the horse to buck its rider off.

Then he compares his hoped-for kingdom to the roan horse he is about to mount into battle: '*this roan shall be my throne*'. This possible link through the generations suggests a new, deeper meaning of the words Richard III made so famous, '*A horse! A horse! My kingdom for a horse!*'

There's something significant about symbols, horses, kingdoms, and leadership to be found buried in this sequence of uncanny 'coincidences'. First recall Richard II (in one of the most surreal scenes in Shakespeare) compares his supplanted kingdom to his beloved roan horse '*jauncing Bolingbroke*', the supplanter, is now riding. This beloved roan horse is a symbol of his reigning over what once was Richard's kingdom. Then as we just saw, the wannabe supplanter of Bolingbroke's kingdom, compares his hoped-for kingdom to the roan horse he is about to mount into battle: '*this roan shall be my throne*'.

Generations later, Richard III, the supplanter of the same kingdom, is dismounted (from his symbolic 'throne') in a losing battle and cries, '*A horse! A horse. My kingdom for a horse!*' What's easy to assume, is the tyrant will do anything to save his own life – even give away his kingdom (assuming all he needs to retain it is a fresh horse).

What's easy to overlook, is when Richard III is immediately offered a new horse, he eschews it. It's as if his squire, Catesby, has misunderstood him. Richard replies, '*Slave, I have set my life upon a cast and I will stand the hazard of the die. I think there be six Richmonds in the field: five I have slain today instead of him. A horse! A horse! My kingdom for a horse!*' – *Richard III*, Act 5, Scene 4.

Those are his last words before he is killed.

Rather than a desperate bid to save his life at any cost, could this be his 'Lear moment'? Is he having an awakening and a repentance? Consider the context.

The night before the battle, Richard III had his Scrooge-like dream where the ghosts of all his murdered victims bring threat of this day's reckoning to his soul. When he awakens shaken, foreshadowing his demise and he gasps, '*Give me another horse. Bind up my wounds. Have mercy Jesu. Soft! I did dream. O coward conscience, how dost thou afflict me!*' – *Richard III*, Act 5, Scene 3.

Is this final moment where he realises what a mistake he's made – he confused his horse, symbol of his *outer* kingdom, with what he (and everybody at a soul-level) really wants – '*another horse*', the true *inner* kingdom, the kingdom of heaven?

Banish False Self, Banish the World

After his father dies and passes the mantle of king to him, Henry, acknowledges his outer journey while strongly alluding to his inner spiritual connection to the waters.

'*The tide of blood in me hath proudly flow'd in vanity till now. Now doth it turn and ebb back to the sea, where it shall mingle with the state of floods, and flow henceforth in formal majesty.*' – Henry V, *Henry IV Part 2* , Act 5, Scene 2.

Initiation is just the beginning of the inner work we need to do to return home to the Soul realm without karma pulling us back to the earth. The bulk of this work is discerning the difference between our twin false selves (good and evil) and the true self they are pretending to be.

After Hal takes his first step away from his 'false name' towards claiming his Truth as Prince Harry, he too has two false selves to deal with. One is represented by his guilt-ridden, insomniac father, Henry IV. The other, of course, is the insidiously lovable rogue, Falstaff. If they represent the Cain–Abel duality, who represents who? Because Falstaff is such an appealing, award-winning buffoon, it's tempting to place Henry Bolingbroke in the central archetype 'I am afraid I am evil'. And Falstaff in 'I pretend to be good'. But this won't wash. First, Bolingbroke does repent, is forgiven, and does see the light — as many of Shakespeare's tragic heroes do at their end. But psycho-spiritually, we take on the pain of feeling guilty because we believe this is a sign of being good. Bad people, after all, do not feel guilt or remorse over their actions, do they?

On the other hand, Falstaff is utterly incorrigible. His soul is a total stranger to his fat head. He is an empty vessel strutting and posturing his way through a fallow life.

Falstaff: Beware the Antichrist

Once we look through the new paradigm, it's pretty obvious that Shakespeare has named Falstaff with the false self-archetype at front of mind. Falstaff — False-Staff — False-Self — False Name. The word *Staff* is also another biblical term for *the waters*, the Sound and Name of God, the Word (*'Thy rod and thy staff [light and sound] do comfort me'* — Psalm 21) — a symbol that returns with great import in the hands of Prospero.

The degree to which we judge, hate and despise the Iago within ourselves, is the degree to which we idolise the inner Falstaff. One of the points made in the Prodigal Son parable is that the father has two sons, one is sinful and 'evil', the other is righteous and 'good'. The 'good' son judges the 'evil' brother and resents his return home — but the father loves them both equally! We are the father to our two inner brothers, Iago and Falstaff. It is impossible for us to be happy and fulfilled in this life (let alone liberate ourselves from endless reincarnation) unless we accept, forgive, and love all aspects of our multi-dimensional nature — unconditionally.

False Staff: False Name

This understanding does not bode well for our rotund rascal. Has Shakespeare seemingly given him 'the false name of God', Lucifer, Satan, Hell, Night ... the Antichrist?

Has our young, unloved, rejected Harry also adopted a false name, a false staff, Hal, that also sounds disconcertingly like 'Hell'? Are then Falstaff and Hal, mirrors of each other and shadows of Prince Harry, his true name?

What, then, does Hal think of his namesake?

It's one thing for Hal to *seem to be* jesting when he accuses Falstaff of being a servant of the devil, '*Thou art violently carried away from grace. There is a devil haunts thee in the likeness of an old fat man.*' But Shakespeare never wastes a single word. They each have a purpose. What, in Falstaff's behaviour, evidences this indictment as a characterisation of Satan himself? Let me count the ways ...

My favourite (of so many) is possibly this. The quality of *honour* that Henry stands for, lives for, and represents, is disdained by the ignorant, hollow cranium of the False Staff. For he's a jolly good fellow ... a jolly dangerous fellow. An Iago is an obvious snake, but the Falstaff is a viper hiding in the roses. As Lady Macbeth goads her husband into murder, she entreats him to '*Look like the innocent flower, but be the serpent under't.*' — *Macbeth*, Act I, Scene 5.

Falstaff *is* such a camouflaged serpent. And, as Jesus banishes Satan from his consciousness, so must Henry banish Falstaff from his and we from ours.

Falstaff on Honour

On the run up to the battle with Hotspur, here's Falstaff's risible discourse on the value of honour.

'Well, 'tis no matter; honour pricks me on. Yea, but how if honour prick me off when I come on? How then? Can honour set-to a leg? No. Or an arm? No. Or take away the grief of a wound? No. Honour hath no skill in surgery, then? No. What is honour? A word. What is in that word 'honour'? What is that 'honour'? Air. A trim reckoning! Who hath it? He that died o'Wednesday. Doth he feel it? No. Doth he hear it? No. 'Tis insensible then? Yea, to the dead. But will it not live with the living? No. Why? Detraction will not suffer it. Therefore I'll none of it. Honour is a mere scutcheon [ornament]. And so ends my catechism.' — Henry IV Part 1, Act 5, Scene I.

Catechism? An elementary book containing a summary of the principles of the Christian religion. Antichrist? I rest my case.

Even in his time, Falstaff was profoundly worshiped by the populous. It is rumoured, Queen Elizabeth I, totally 'seduced' by him, pressured Shakespeare into resurrecting him in *The Merry Wives of Windsor*.

To this day, such is the lure of the False Staff within us, he is still idolised by directors and top actors alike. When we have such awesome actors as, say, Simon Russell-Beale and Anthony Sher enfolding their selves around the False Staff, what's essentially appalling becomes irresistibly appealing. If Falstaff is an even more insidious enemy of the soul than Iago or Richard III, would it not be interesting to violate tradition and the sacred pig and see what happens if we play him as dark as Iago or Lady Macbeth?

Humour: An Attribute of God

Having said that, one of the best ways to spiritualise a situation is bring humour and joy into it. When my clients get stuck, unable to entreat my horses even to move, it's often because they are treating the horses in the arena like they do the guys at the office — too damn seriously. When they find ways to let go and play naturally and spontaneously the horses will join in. Seemingly impossible results, become *I'm possible*.

Likewise, religious approaches tend towards the sanctimonious and the serious. Monty Python horrified the Church by seeing the funny side of the crucifixion with the ditty-with-the-truism *Always look on the bright side of life*. But Jesus got the last laugh on his killers by rising up again the next day! Is this what Shakespeare is doing here? When Falstaff who, as if he hasn't already proven how utterly lacking in honour, integrity, principle, truth ... performs a pantomime, a farce, a mocking parody of the biblical story of the crucifixion and resurrection of Christ! Shakespeare is pushing the already-stretched heretical envelope to bursting point with this playful Christ motif.

During the battle, unable to avoid fighting someone, Falstaff falls down and plays possum until his bewildered foe departs. While still feigning death, with one eye open, he witnesses Henry killing Hotspur. Henry spies what he believes to be his fat corpse lying there and offers a sarcastic 'eulogy' over it. *'What, old acquaintance! Could not all this flesh keep in a little life? Poor Jack, farewell! I could have better spar'd a better man.'* – Henry IV Part 1, Act 5, Scene 4.

When Henry has left the scene, Falstaff 'resurrects'! Uttering one of the most oft quoted lines in the English tongue, *'The better part of valour is discretion'*. Possessing neither quality, he then goes over to the corpse of Hotspur and lances him in the thigh, mocking the act of the centurion Longinus, at the crucifixion. Having 'killed him again', he takes Hotspur's twice-dead body on his back and, on meeting the much-confused Prince Harry, claims the kill for himself, and demands an honour from the king for his valour. Henry generously – unattached to the gory glory – gives way to the incorrigible lying tub of lard, *'For my part, if a lie may do thee grace, I'll gild it with the happiest terms I have ... the day is ours.'* In the spirit of the authentic leader he is becoming, he also offers mercy and grace to his defeated enemies.

The Boar's Head

Shakespeare must have enjoyed thinking up the name for the Inn in which Falstaff makes a pig of himself and drags Hal down into the low life with him. He calls it the Boar's Head. A delightful pun around Falstaff's boorish nature and an allusion to the biblical Prodigal son's desperately squalid abode – the pig sty – before finally returning home to his father. *'Prodigals lately come from swine-keeping, from eating draff and husks.'* Quoth Falstaff, least we miss his subtleties. It's highly probable that the Inn, the Boar's Head, also symbolises the *Inn of the Nativity* that in its turn symbolises the domain of the false self that has *'no room within'* for the Christ!

Forgiveness and Inner Peace

As we've already said, and some things improve with repetition, God does not judge, God's entire being is the essence of forgiveness, mercy, and compassion. That's why we cannot enter the kingdom of God with our burdens of guilt and resentment on our backs. The camel must bow its knees. We must forgive ourselves and (and this is the paradigm shift) the judgments we hold toward others. We cannot forgive 'them'. But if we want inner peace, we can let go the toxic feelings we have about 'them' that are poisoning our own blood. As acclaimed novelist Henry Miller articulates so beautifully:

'I know what the great cure is: it is to give up, to relinquish, to surrender, so that our little hearts may beat in unison with the great heart of the world.'

When Hal became Prince Harry, stepped up and supported his father in defending his crown against the Hotspur, it began the process of healing their relationship and bridging the cold chasm of separation between them.

Whereas Falstaff and everything shallow and phony he represented was incorrigible, Bolingbroke, already an ill man, wanted nothing more than to die in peace and be forgiven for what he saw as his sin and his crime.

In a very touching scene, Bolingbroke is near his end enjoying the first decent sleep he's had in years, and Harry comes to sit beside him. He sees his crown significantly lying on the pillow beside his sleeping head.

'*Why doth the crown lie there upon his pillow, being so troublesome a bedfellow? O polished perturbation! Golden care! Sleep with it now!*' – Henry IV Part 2, Act 4, Scene 5.

Taking up the crown and trying it on, he expresses his love for his father, sadness at the inevitable loss, and pride at the honour of wearing it.

'*Thy due from me is tears and heavy sorrows of the blood which nature, love, and filial tenderness, shall O dear father, pay thee plentiously. My due from thee is this imperial crown, which as immediate from thy place and blood, derives itself to me.[Putting on the crown] Lo where it sits — which God shall guard; and put the world's whole strength into one giant arm, it shall not force this lineal honour from me.*'

In a disturbing twist, Bolingbroke awakens to find his crown missing and Harry, having left the bedchamber. He jumps to the wrong conclusion – that Harry couldn't wait for him to be dead – because he hates his father so much! Confronting him, he spits:

'*Thou hid'st a thousand daggers in my thoughts, which thou hast whetted on thy stony heart, to stab at half an hour of my life. What, canst thou not forbear me half an hour? Then get thee gone, and dig my grave thyself.*'

Harry drops to his knee in humility and begs his father hear his reason.

'*God witness with me, when I here came in and found no course of breath within your majesty, how cold it struck my heart!*'

Henry IV's Blessing

As they reconcile, and Bolingbroke dies in a symbolic Jerusalem (City of Peace), he releases the burden of his ill-gotten crown, that uneasy did he wear upon his head, and blesses Henry's reign, '*How I came by the crown, O God, forgive; and grant it may with thee in true peace live!*' – Henry IV Part 2, Act 4, Scene 5.

Harry responds with, '*My gracious liege, you won it, wore it, gave it me; then plain and right must my possession be; which I with more than with a common pain 'gainst all the world will rightfully maintain.*'

Nota Bene: that recurring phrase '*all the world*'. All the world means Satan.

As soon as he is crowned the fifth Henry, he has unfinished business to dispatch.

In the much earlier 'charade scene', set in the Boar's Head (prodigal's pig sty), Shakespeare foreshadows the banishment of Falstaff. Hal and Falstaff take turns in role-playing how the king would view their friendship.

Hal, having played a prank on Falstaff, outs him as an out-and-out liar and a fool prior to unravelling the quagmire of sands upon which he has built the hollow man to play opposite Bolingbroke's hollow crown.

'*These lies are like the father that begets them, gross as a mountain, open, palpable. Why thy clay-brained guts, thou knotty-pated fool, thou whoreson obscene greasy tallow-catch.*' – Henry IV Part 1, Act 2, Scene 4.

As Lear's false-self Regan sagely says, '*Jesters do oft prove prophets,*'!

In character as his father talking to him, Hal, jesting, pretends to read Falstaff's I Ching, '*Swearest Thou? Ungracious boy, henceforth ne'er look on me. Thou art violently carried away from grace. There is a devil haunts thee in the likeness of an old fat man. A tun of man is thy companion. Why dost Thou converse with that trunk of humors, that bolting-hutch of beastliness, that swollen parcel of dropsies, that huge bombard of sack, that stuffed cloakbag of guts, that roasted Manningtree ox with the pudding in his belly, that reverend Vice, that gray iniquity, that father ruffian, that vanity in years? Wherein is he good, but to taste sack and drink it? Wherein neat and cleanly but to carve a capon and eat it? Wherein cunning but in craft? Wherein crafty but in villainy? Wherein villainous but in all things? Wherein worthy but in nothing?'*

Now Falstaff rises to his own defence, deploying his vast arsenal of emotionally-manipulating weapons. So effective is Falstaff's appeal as a character, (just as our false selves do) he takes on a life of his own, almost independent of Shakespeare. Like Frankenstein's monster, an unstoppable force is unleashed, unwittingly into the world. Only the hardest-hearted would fail to shed a tear for poor, old, hard-done-by, Jack ...

'But to say I know more harm in him than in myself were to say more than I know. That he is old, the more the pity; his white hairs do witness it. But that he is, saving your reverence, a whoremaster, that I utterly deny. If sack and sugar be a fault, God help the wicked. If to be old and merry be a sin, then many an old host that I know is damned. If to be fat be to be hated, then Pharaoh's lean kine are to be loved. No, my good lord, banish Peto, banish Bardolph, banish Poins, but for sweet Jack Falstaff, kind Jack Falstaff, true Jack Falstaff, valiant Jack Falstaff, and therefore more valiant being, as he is old Jack Falstaff, banish not him thy Harry's company. Banish plump Jack, and banish all the world.'

Sound familiar? We've recently seen Emilia, Iago's wife confess she'd sell her honour for nothing less than '*all the world*'. This is a motif that reminds us of the temptation that Jesus did not fall for, and was his last test before vanquishing Satan in the wilderness. Now Hal is being seduced by the same temptation not through greed, but through emotional blackmail, through the apotheosis of sympathy-leeching falsehood – Falstaff.

Here lie the twin forks of the enemy of the soul. One fork is the mind: the endless churning of imponderable questions; the constant pseudo-intellectualisation; the insatiable demand for proof, logic, sense and reason; the sneering disdain for natural knowing and intuition; the need for masculine force to be dominant and make might right, the desperation for a sense of importance and superiority that compulsively criticises and puts others down.

The other fork is the emotional Corryvreckan maelstrom, the whirlpool of lies and tyrannies of weakness that tumble out of the false self's mouth to make Niagara Falls look like a mere teardrop.

Falstaff seduces us, and we love him. But Hal banishes him, and for a while, we are torn between our love and admiration for this David, this boy turned warrior king, and the shock we feel at the harsh treatment he seems to dish out to his old friends.

The understanding only comes when we ourselves banish the 'character' from our vision, and see them as archetypes inhabiting our own psyches.

Now the prophecy is made manifest.

Falstaff, on hearing of Henry's coronation, seizes the moment he has been anticipating for many years, to bask in the royal glow. But Henry does not shine on him. *'Presume not,'* he rebukes Falstaff, *'that I am the thing I was, for God doth know, so the world perceive, that I have turn'd away my former self; so will I those that kept me company',* and banishes Falstaff on pain of death.

This Henry has ruthlessly to do. Falstaff is not a real person. He represents the delusion within Henry that will anchor him to his past like a sunken galley. What Henry does with Falstaff is what we all must do to our delusions and addictions if we're going to follow the same path as Henry.

The Law of Return

'Fortune made his sword; by which the world's best garden he achieved.' – *Henry V*, Act 5, Scene 2.

Have you ever given up a bad habit and suddenly found you've put back all the weight or taken up smoking again without fully realising how it happened?

That's the law of return. Whenever we change a pattern, sometime later, when we are feeling relaxed and confident, we get tested. Have we really learned the lesson? Have we really cleared the pattern? If you're on the way of the warrior, these tests are as inevitable as they are ruthless.

Now Henry is the resurrected Richard, his goal is to ascend the brightest heaven of invention – Eden. We've enjoyed Eden played by England, Scotland, and Belmont, now it's France's turn to play Eden and the Dauphin's (Prince of France's) turn to play Hotspur, the former rival for the Grail when Henry was still the young Prince of Wales.

Clear Intention

If you were a true spiritual warrior setting out on a war to conquer France, a quest where, not only your destiny and life were at stake, but also the lives of countless others, before embarking on it, would you not make sure your intention was clear, was legally sanctioned, and spiritually supported?

The first step Henry takes looks to history, convoluted, maybe spurious, and disingenuous, but metaphorically to us, it's spot on. Shakespeare inveigles none other than The Archbishop of Canterbury (as a symbol of spirituality – '*We of the spirituality will raise your highness such a mighty sum as never did the clergy at one time bring in to any of your ancestors*') to make sure his claim to the throne of France is legal, sanctioned by God, and he has a right to return home to 'the world's best garden', our Garden of Eden. He has seen first-hand the fate that befalls the usurper. He's not going to supplant the throne of France as a Satan. As an Adam, he is going to reclaim his long-lost, rightful, kingdom – the kingdom of heaven.

'O for a muse of fire, that would ascend the brightest heaven of invention.' – Prologue, Henry V.

The Archbishop reminds us how far Henry has come, 'The breath no sooner left his father's body but that his wildness, mortified in him, seem'd to die too; yea, at that very moment, consideration like an angel came and whipp'd th' offending Adam out of him, leaving his body as a paradise t' envelop and contain celestial spirits.'

The Archbishop possesses not the wit to comprehend Harry's transformation from 'offending Adam' to ascended master – but as long as we do, that's all that matters.

However, the Archbishop does use the book of Numbers in the bible to cement the case for Harry's claim by tracing how France has deviously and inaptly used Salic Law to usurp the throne rightfully due to England. Harry goes to great pains to reassure us he's, ' ... no tyrant, but a Christian king, unto whose grace is as subject as are our wretches fett'red in our prisons', a muse of fire, an Adam, who in God's name is ousting the usurper who supplanted his throne. He warns Canterbury not to doctor the evidence supporting this claim – on pain of divine retribution, 'How you awaken our sleeping sword of war – we charge you, in the name of God, take heed.' – Henry V, Act I, Scene 2.

Just like the story of David confronting Goliath, Shakespeare repeatedly makes the point that Harry puts, not just 'God' but 'God's Name' before him. Through this key, he challenges the spirit in all ways, and affirms his intention, 'Now we are well resolv'd; and by God's help, and yours, the noble sinews of our power, France being ours, we'll bend it to our awe ... '

The Judas Motif

'Nay, but the man that was his bedfellow, whom he hath dull'd and cloy'd with gracious favours, that he should, for a foreign purse, so sell his sovereign's life to death and treachery.' – Exeter, *Henry V*, Act 2, Scene 2.

As Henry embarks on his campaign to restore the Grail of France he is apprised of a betrayal by three traitors, one of whom is a close 'bedfellow', Scroop. How we deal with our own disloyalty to our soul is one of the essential ingredients in our spiritual transformation. The play is a drama, so we can expect Shakespeare to exaggerate for effect, but if we look in Genesis at the God character's reaction towards the serpent and the Adam–Eve after their betrayal of man, Henry's tirade to Scroop after his disloyalty is unearthed is a pretty accurate reimagining of that fateful moment and a harsh echo of Isaiah's prophesy of Lucifer's downfall:

'How art thou fallen from heaven, O Lucifer, son of the morning! how art thou cut down to the ground, which didst weaken the nations!' – Isaiah 14:12

Shakespeare deliciously establishes the traitors as having a 'Shylock's' (Cain's) lack of mercy and thirst for punishment. He offers them the same choice – grace or rude will. He brings upon the traitorous trio the irony of the same judgment they would mete out themselves. He upgrades 'thirty pieces of silver' into 'Gold' (the selfsame metal).

And finally, through Henry, he builds in the motif of the Angry Christ who upturned the satanic tables in the temple – while simultaneously confirming our theory and linking all the way back to Richard II betrayed by his own father, and dubbed *'a second fall of cursed man'* by his queen. Read or watch the entire speech and you can feel the reckoning of God coming down, not on man, but on Satan – before he is (ultimately) forgiven, of course!

It's not hard to spot the resounding similarity to Isaiah's prophesy of the vanquishing of Lucifer with another of Henry's famous tongue-lashings.

'But, O, What shall I say to thee, Lord Scroop? thou cruel, ingrateful, savage and inhuman creature! Thou that didst bear the key of all my counsels, that knew'st the very bottom of my soul, that almost mightst have coin'd me into gold … With some suspicion. I will weep for thee; for this revolt of thine, methinks, is like another fall of man.' – Henry V, Act 2, Scene 2.

Of course, the insult he affords Scroop is to cast him into the bottomless pit in the company of Caliban, and Iago's 'monstrous birth'.

The Nails of the Crucifixion Motif

In my foreword I warned you I was squeezing in more ingredients as they jumped out at me while watching the movie again. This one is exquisite. In arguably the most excruciating, least necessary, scene in the canon, the French Princess Catherine receives an English lesson from her lady-in-waiting, Alice. The superficial implication is she wants to know how to say in English various parts of the body of her prospective husband, Henry V.

Why?

In our paradigm, this allusion to 'the body' becomes to '*the body of Christ*'. In this short scene beginning with Catherine (speaking entirely in French), '*Je te prie, m'enseignez; il faut que j'apprenne à parler. Comment appelez-vous la main en Anglois ?*', she demands first to know the word for the hand of her groom, fair enough. But the words 'hand' and 'nails' are then repeated a not insignificant eighteen times! I wonder why?

Once again we can see Shakespeare using scenes in his plays as a vehicle to dramatise symbols of the Old Testament prophesies. Prophesies that somehow delineate absolutely, precisely, what Jesus has to do or have done to him – not to prove he was the Messiah – but to fulfil the law and restore the soul to its rightful seat. The law has been fulfilled – whether we know it or believe it or like it or not – that's what Shakespeare is telling us. It is done. Thy will be done.

'*For dogs have compassed me: the assembly of the wicked have inclosed me: they pierced my hands and my feet.*' – Psalm 22:16.

The scene ends (mercifully) with Catherine calling God's name (O Lord God) and giving a recap of the names she has learned for the crucial body parts of, erm, Jesus?

'*Le foot et le count! O Seigneur Dieu! Ils sont les mots de son mauvais, corruptible, gros, et impudique, et non pour les dames de honneur d'user. Je ne voudrais prononcer ces mots devant les seigneurs de France pour tout le monde. Foh! Le foot et le count! Néanmoins, je réciterai une autre fois ma leçon ensemble: d'hand, de fingre, de nailès, d'arma, d'elbow, de nick, de sin, de foot, le count.*' – Catherine, *Henry V*, Act 3, Scene 4.

The Massacre of the Innocents Motiff

'*Kill the poys and the luggage! 'Tis expressly against the law of arms. 'Tis as arrant a piece of knavery, mark you now, as can be offert, in your conscience now, is it not?*' – Fluellen.

It was Herod who, with callous indifference, infamously slaughtered the innocents in the Christ nativity story. Although outwardly such an act violates every nerve and cell in our body, inwardly it resonates with the true outrage at how Satan murders the soul – every time we deny or forget who we really are. This suffering is what we are inflicting on ourselves every day. Do we feel it? Not any more. It has become our normal state, our numbed out background pain. As I reach for my morning coffee, or my evening glass of wine, I am simply trying to find a way to cope with a pain inside that has no feelings, no words, not even a thought left to make sense of it.

Shakespeare is reminding us of this every time he builds in a scene where we witness atrocity, savagery and violation of the innocent. In *Titus Andronicus* he pushes us to our very limit with the violation of Lavinia, brutally raped and disfigured by Chiron and Demetrius. Here, he shakes us awake when the French act out the Herod Motif and pointlessly slaughter the young boys who are simply minding the luggage.

Impeccable Leadership

We can never vanquish our false selves entirely. We need them. Not to run our lives for us, but to serve our higher purpose. The aim of *authentic leadership development* is to educate our false selves and take leadership authority over them. However, they often shape-shift into more subtle — or more threatening — guises. They have a job to do — temper our steel, hone our blade, and strengthen our arm, so we can cut away the shadows, lies and illusions. Far better to be disillusioned, than deluded.

In our Harry's case Shakespeare has Hotspur 'resurrect' as Lewis (sic), the Dauphin of France, to wage the inner war on his soul. When he hears of Harry's claim on the French throne, Lewis sends him a gift. Through his ambassador he needles Harry by attempting to trigger his former prodigal self, '*You savour too much of your youth, and bids you be advis'd there's nought in France that can be with a nimble galliard [dance] won.*' The gift is a chest of tennis balls! He is mocking the king. His is the voice of the false self that continually undermines us. It is a voice that Harry heeds not. He sends back a chilling message, '*His jest will savour but of shallow wit, when thousands weep more than did laugh at it.*' Harry passes his first test. The Dauphin has caught the tiger by the tail. '*When the blast of war blows in our ears, imitate the action of the tiger.*' — *Henry V*, Act 3, Scene I.

Ruthless Cutting by the Sword of Truth

Although Falstaff is now dead, the traces and scars of Harry's life with him still need to be healed. He's already vowed to banish all those associated with his former self. These traces are represented by his former friends, Pistol, Bardolph and Nym. Pistol marries Mistress Quickly, Falstaff's widow. She soon dies ignominiously of the pox. Bardolph, a notorious thief, is hanged on Exeter's orders for looting after Harfleur. Harry seems unmoved. Then Nym, significantly, is also caught looting and the sentencing passes to the king. Significant, because Nym means 'Name'. Is Nym the trace left by the False Staff, the false name Harry must be ruthless in cutting away? To symbolise this ruthless quality of the Spiritual Warrior, Harry too sentences his old friend Nym to death by hanging. Seems callous, cold-hearted, uncaring? Yes, it does. We, to liberate the soul, must all too often find the inner strength to risk disapproval and judgment by those who cannot see the spiritual wood for the worldly trees.

Harry's ability to tune into the spiritual vision of the seagull, always present, always available to those with the eyes to see and the ears to hear, is keenly demonstrated in his leadership before, during and after his Goliath, Agincourt.

In yet another of the most famous lines in all literature, before Harfleur Harry puts 'God's Name' ahead, '*Follow your spirit; and upon this charge cry God for Harry, England and Saint George!*' – *Henry V*, Act 3, Scene 1.

In the prelude to Agincourt, through Exeter the Dauphin is given this stern blow from the sword of truth, and we are given another foreshadowing of Prospero and the mystical Sound Current of his Tempest, '*Therefore in fierce tempest is he coming, in thunder and in earthquake, like a Jove*'. And, lest we doubt or forget, to remind us of the symbolism of the tempest as a representation of the waters, Shakespeare has the

King of France play this back to us in the following scene. *'For England his approaches makes as fierce as waters to the sucking of a gulf.' – Henry V*, Act 2, Scene 4.

Agincourt: David fells Goliath – Adam Overcomes Lucifer

Henry V's Agincourt was Shakespeare's holy war. There's an ancient sacred Hebrew saying, *'Baruch Bashan'* meaning 'the blessings already are'. Who we really are is already perfect. All we really need we already have within us.

Before the battle, all the English soldiers could see was how small their numbers were, how desperately they erroneously believed they needed those men left behind in England (defending the lands against a Scottish invasion). All they could see was doom, all they could feel was hopeless fear.

Understanding this, first he prays to the God of battles. He asks again for forgiveness for the sins of his father in falsely compassing the crown. He clears his own consciousness and realigns himself with the God within and his higher purpose.

This inspires him to walk in disguise amongst the common men to gauge the true pulse of his army unsullied by their need to sacrifice their honesty to look 'respectful' to the king.

Finally, to align his army with his own spiritually ordained purpose, he takes the truth of the situation to cut away the fears and reframes facing impossible odds into an opportunity for more true inner glory and honour than they ever imagined possible. *'If we are marked to die, we are enow to do our country loss; and if to live the fewer men, the greater the share of honour.' – Henry V*, Act 4, Scene 3.

In a sweet reprise of Portia's three caskets (lead, silver, and gold) he reminds us and his trembling troops who he is not, *'By Jove, I am not covetous for gold, nor care I* who feeds upon my cost; it yearns me not if men my garments wear; such outward things dwell not in my desires. But if it be a sin to covet honour, I am the most offending soul alive.' Shakespeare emphasises that Harry is the antithesis of his 'False Staff' because Falstaff cannot understand the notion of true self-sacrifice, he so disdains 'honour' that he calls it nothing more than an ornament, 'Honour is a mere scutcheon.' – Henry IV pt.I, Act 5, Scene I.

Harry's famous 'band of brothers' line is an unprecedented invocation for a true (resurrected) king. Shakespeare, never one to miss an opportunity to resonate with Christ-like motifs, is effectively connecting at a true, soul level honouring the oneness of all in the Kingdom of God and the brotherhood of Man, 'We few, we happy few, we band of brothers; for he today that sheds his blood with me shall be my brother; be he ne'er so vile.'

The rest, as they say, is history (with a touch of creative license). Immediately, they are told the day is won, in a clear mirror of the biblical David story, Harry acknowledges the true spiritual warrior who vanquishes the forces of darkness, the name of God. He entreats his 'brothers' to chant in unison the 'Non Nobis', 'Non nobis, domine, non nobis, sed nomini tua da gloriam.' ('Not unto us, O Lord, not unto us, but to thy name give the glory.')

In God's Name?

What does this mean? What does it really mean to put God's name ahead, and to glorify God's name? The hidden Truth of this has been completely supplanted in our consciousness with all manner of false teachings. What was heresy then, still is to this day. But it's very clear Shakespeare knows the Truth here. The name is the Word, the sound of the soul. To 'glorify the name' means to use it for what it is intended. It is a practical spirituality that anyone can employ. It is freely available to all. We can all simply ask *'for the light to go ahead of us for the highest good of all concerned'*. At any time, we can all intone the sacred name (the 'hu'), spiritualise our consciousness and invoke spiritual guidance and protection.

Whether the 'historical' Henry V did all this, who knows. But Shakespeare's *Henry V* certainly seems to be demonstrating to us all the core principles of practicing the Sound Current.

Historical accounts of Agincourt say the body count was around 30,000 French and 6,000 English. Shakespeare calls the number of English dead as *'But five and twenty'*. This is a subtle way of heralding the miracle of the end of Satan's choke-hold over man!

Numerology is a practice that adds the individual figures in a number to get the meaning of the 'inner number'. In this case $25 = 2 + 5 = 7$. Seven is an ubiquitous biblical number symbolising 'completeness and perfection'. Cryptic sevens are found everywhere in sacred writings: traps for the unwary. From the seven days in Genesis to the seven seals in Revelation.

What do we make of this in the context of the spiritual journey we have now made through Henry, as Adam, as the soul, as the Christ within? How does this sign hang on this momentous line from his uncle Exeter, extolling the courage shown by York in the battle in which he fell: *'And so, espous'd to death, with blood he seal'd a testament of noble-ending love.'* He's referring to the revelation that Jesus, as the Christ, sealed the New Testament in his blood — and in so doing overcame *'all the world'* of Satan and fulfilled the Law of Moses.

Adam Reuniting with his Eve

On regaining his Eden, he seals his new realm by marrying Catherine, the Princess of France with a blessing – not as we'd expect from her father, the king – but from her mother, the Queen.

'God, the best maker of all marriages, combine your hearts in one, your realms in one! As man and wife, being two, are one in love, so be there 'twixt your kingdom such a spousal that never may ill office or fell jealousy.' – *Henry V*, Act 5, Scene 2.

We're seeing the unlikely becoming the most probable. The unrelated, strange coincidences in the plots becoming carefully orchestrated chains of events. So can our certainty grow another bud towards it full blossoming? Certainty that Shakespeare is ending his saga of a deposed and murdered rightful king (Richard II) reborn in spirit as the wayward prince, son of the usurping kingslayer. A 'muse of such fire' that can transcend the gravity of his illusory selves and as Jesus the Christ is said to have done, overcome the world of lies and illusion. The Christ that is in Harry and in all of us opened the way for all mankind to break out of the 'prison' that Richard was martyred in. Recall Richard compare his prison to 'the world', on behalf of all souls on earth, *'How may I compare the prison where I live unto the world?'* Hamlet used the same imagery when he also compared Denmark (and the whole world) to a prison.

Through Harry, Shakespeare is urging us to invoke the 'ascended' soul within ourselves. This is the sleeping hero, the resurrected soul of Adam, within us all. As our true self, the true Henry V, the resurrected Richard, symbol of Adam, we can pass though the opening, the way to the kingdom.

Recall the words of Richard's queen as Shakespeare entreats us, his disciples, to fly like the seagull to see the patterns, the harmony, the perfect design,

169

the unfathomable love holding all of us and everything together as one living, breathing thought in the mind of what we call God — without, in the mind, being able to comprehend what this really is?

'Thou, old Adam's likeness, set to dress this garden how dares thy harsh tongue sound this unpleasing news? What Eve, what serpent, hath suggested thee to make a second fall of cursed man?' — *Richard II*, Act 3, Scene 4.

And as the end of the circle of life is also its beginning, let's remember, as we were banished, so we return home: *'This star of England. Fortune made his sword; by which the world's best garden he achieved.'* — *Henry V*, Act 5, Scene 2.

PART 3
SHAKESPEARE'S REVELATION

CHAPTER SIX
Hamlet

'To Be, or Not To Be: That is the (Only) Question.'

S ince George Bernard Shaw famously said, '*All great truths begin as blasphemies*', I sincerely hope I am about to join the ranks of history's great blasphemers and that my liver will be put to good use after I die.

'*To be or not to be*' was the original choice given by God to Mankind, represented by Adam in the Beginning.' This is why it is still the only question worth asking of ourselves every moment of every day. That is why this speech is still as alive today as it was in Shakespeare's day, as it was in the Beginning, as it will be till the End. It is indelibly etched into the very fabric of our soul. This is why the effect of hearing this is like the voice of God calling on us to wake up and come home.

In my 30s I fantasised about playing *Hamlet* at the RSC. The closest I got was performing the '*to be, or not to be*' soliloquy at a personal development workshop called 'The Mastery'. Now in my Lear Years, I shall offer the part to you – whether or not you play it at the RSC.

If you go to my website at www.ShakespearesRevelation.com, you'll find details of coaching programmes and workshops based on the principles of the existential choice: '*To be, or not to be?*' developed here. A choice we have available to us every moment.

Journal work for this chapter could include contemplating the question: who am I really? Imagine you are Hamlet. You have lost not only your true father and your mother to a tyrant, but you've lost the presence of God in your heart. You've lost paradise and perfection. You've lost the song of love in your ears that, wherever you may roam or whenever you feel lost, will draw you home with music.

As you follow Hamlet as he reclaims his birthright, ask yourself what are you willing to do, to confront, to sacrifice, in order to regain what is truly yours — inside your consciousness.

The big question here is when you choose not *to be* (and become negative, resentful, vindictive, etc) how instead could you choose *to be* (accepting, forgiving, loving) in the face of the temptation to act against yourself or others? Turn the other cheek, perhaps?

What aspects of your soul-self (Ophelia) do you deny or banish from your life? For what reason? Does any reason really justify that?

We've seen thus far how the mille feuilles of Shakespeare's plays enable us to enjoy three key levels of narrative:

∾ Physical story

∾ Psycho-spiritual allegory

∾ Mystical–theological discourse

As we gaze into the penultimate facet of Shakespeare's diamond he begins to make the mystical dimension of his work come to the fore. He pulls together some deeper threads from other plays and prepares us for the mystical travels we are soon to take to Prospero's mysterious Isle and Shakespeare's final revelation.

As we learned from *Macbeth*, his deeper, mystical ingredients are usually found swirling in his cauldron and pay no homage to any chronology – as long as they're in the mix the spell works. This makes making any kind of logical, mentally-satisfying sense of order out of them futile. We still have to transcend the limitations of our minds and allow the intellect of the soul to whisper its truth to us based on the subtle vibrations and images in the verse.

The one ingredient that does help us organise our thoughts is the core distinction clarified in *Hamlet*: *to be*, or not *to be* – what exactly *is* the question?

I'm suggesting this timeless, most precious piece of literature itself plays three roles:

- Sums up the fundamental, hidden, existential, triune choice Shakespeare has been offering us throughout between innocent true self and the two (good–evil) false selves.

- Sets the agenda for Hamlet's allegorical tale.

- Makes Shakespeare's mystical allusions as specific as he dares.

As you read this verse look through the eyes of your own soul and let it be personal, very personal. Imagine it is the voice of Adam within you contemplating the appalling sadness of having made a foolish choice in the beginning and having to live the consequence for an eternity – unless, unless, you can do something to rectify your mistake. Quite a play!

Ask yourself do you want to be (who you really are as a soul) or not? And what are the consequences of choosing either way? The entire play is Hamlet's (ergo Shakespeare's) stunning answer to this question:

'To be or not to be — that is the question:

Whether 'tis nobler in the mind to suffer

The slings and arrows of outrageous fortune,

Or to take arms against a sea of troubles,

And, by opposing, end them. To die, to sleep —

No more — and by a sleep to say we end

The heartache and the thousand natural shocks

That flesh is heir to — 'tis a consummation

Devoutly to be wished. To die, to sleep —

To sleep, perchance to dream. Aye, there's the rub,

For in that sleep of death what dreams may come,

When we have shuffled off this mortal coil,

Must give us pause. There's the respect

That makes calamity of so long life.

For who would bear the whips and scorns of time,

Th' oppressor's wrong, the proud man's contumely,

The pangs of disprised love, the law's delay,

The insolence of office, and the spurns

That patient merit of the unworthy takes,

When he himself might his quietus make

With a bare bodkin? Who would fardels bear,

To grunt and sweat under a weary life,

But that the dread of something after death,

The undiscovered country from whose bourn

No traveller returns, puzzles the will

And makes us rather bear those ills we have

Than fly to others that we know not of?

Thus conscience does make cowards of us all,

And thus the native hue of resolution

Is sicklied o'er with the pale cast of thought,

And enterprises of great pith and moment,

With this regard their currents turn awry,

And lose the name of action. — Soft you now,

The fair Ophelia. — Nymph, in thy orisons

Be all my sins remembered.' — Hamlet, Act 3, Scene I

Soul-Centred View

'Waking up spiritually means becoming more and more aware that, in addition to the horizontal dimension of physical-world reality, there's an enormous vertical direction of spiritual reality that you're also travelling along. It's this upward journey that's the soul's 'learning line' and everyone's purpose in coming to the Earth School.' — Drs, Ron and Mary Hulnick, *Loyalty to Your Soul.*

From our seagull's eye view, Hamlet has awakened from the midsummer night's dream that we all sleep through and realises what has actually happened to his former life where he lived in paradise. Now, as the dawning light shines into his shadows, he is contemplating *three* options:

❧ *To be*:

To ascend to a pure state of being, to accept that what is is, to forgive, to seek the highest good of all concerned, to my own self be true, embody the attributes of the soul, of God ... to let be — the readiness is all ...

❧ Or not *to be*:

To enter the twin forks of the serpent's inescapable dilemma:

∿ To suffer and be a victim or …

∿ To resist, rail against reality, fight – maybe die, maybe kill myself to escape the dilemma …

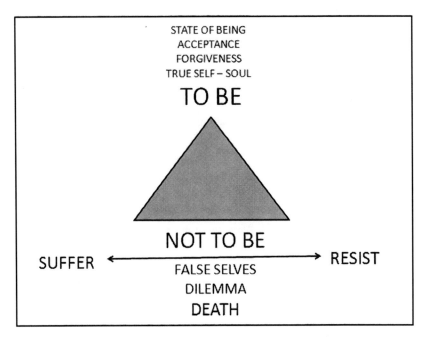

Setting the Scene

To set the scene, let's look inside Hamlet's consciousness, his Denmark. Denmark has now been cast as Eden and we are told in act One, Scene Four that '*Something is rotten in the state of Denmark.*'

This is why, by any other word, it would smell so foul.

On the physical story level, we see Hamlet return home to find his father is dead, his mother Gertrude has immediately married his father's brother, Claudius. Claudius has taken the crown for himself and rules the land in drunken, incestuous revelry. It's a very different world from the one his true father once created.

HAMLET

"This above all; to thine own self be true, and it follows, as the night the day, thou cants't not then be false to any man."

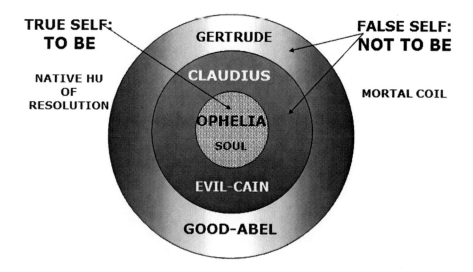

Like Lear's, like ours, Hamlet's inner kingdom is divided into three portions.

The thing about Shakespeare is we're never alone. He has not abandoned us with the secrets of the universe and said *'good luck!'*. He is a master. A spiritual teacher. He is not a religious pundit who proffers pre-digested dogma for us to swallow and obey. We do need to figure it out. That's how we learn and grow as an evolving soul. So we need to ask the right question and the right clue is right here. These are plays. He plays with us. He loves us so much you can feel it in every word he says. He wants us to play with him. With his characters. He wants us to be them. To be Hamlet. This is *Hamlet*. This is Hamlet's inner world. We are Hamlet. This is our inner world. The play is the question – and the answer. So play.

These are the characterisations who populate Hamlet's *inner* world. If we are seduced by the characters and the *outer* game we will lose sight of the spiritual teaching. The only way to get the inner spiritual nourishment is to step away from the outer world and inhale the breath of life Shakespeare breathes into us as did God in the beginning.

Hamlet is Ophelia

Hamlet *is* Ophelia. Ophelia *is* Hamlet's 'to be', his true self. It is to her he prays, referring to her as 'Nymph' is an allusion to her as soul, as God within. This means Hamlet's story is once again the 'Christ's' story and thus our inner story. A story that is his dying wish to be told.

'Nymph, in thy orisons [prayers] be all my sins [ignorance of who I am] remembered.'

Keep your eye on Ophelia. She is the key to understanding *Hamlet* and understanding yourself. The process and symbolism surrounding Ophelia's so-called 'death' is the revelation of Hamlet's own 'death' and resurrection. As we saw in *Macbeth*, Shakespeare hides his secrets like a master impressionist, a brushstroke here and dab or two there. You'll see!

Originally, his inner kingdom was ruled by his father and mother. King Hamlet and Queen Gertrude represent the Adam and the Eve archetypes. His soul (Ophelia) to whom he has just prayed, asking for his 'sins' to be forgiven, is enslaved by two impostors, the Serpent (Cain) and his fallen mother (Abel).

When his father's ghost appears (Adam) and tells him he was in fact murdered by Claudius (Serpent) Hamlet is called to avenge his father's death and his mother's betrayal.

'But howsoever thou pursuest this act, taint not thy mind: nor let thy soul contrive against thy mother aught; leave her to heaven, and to those thorns that in her bosom lodge, to prick and sting her.' – Hamlet, Act I, Scene 5.

But what does *avenge* really mean? The ghost does not tell Hamlet to kill Claudius. And he demands divine retribution for Gertrude. The assumption in the mind is that avenge means revenge and that revenge means get even and get even means punish and destroy. This is the law of 'an eye for an eye' and, in our gut-level humanness, it's what we all crave as did Shylock. This is the law of the not *to be*. This is where Hamlet plays out the dilemma of man. Not between right and wrong, but between law and grace. The *to be* is hidden by the mortal coil, and the enterprise of great pith and moment is to accept, forgive, and take action in the Name of God – just as Henry V did most of the time.

Shuffle Off Your Mortal Coil

Through the eyes of the soul, the body, imagination, mind, emotions, and unconscious are all different levels of the same vehicle through which it expresses: the mortal coil. The aspect Shakespeare is calling our attention to is the twin false selves, the Cain–Abel that wants to live its life using our soul's energy as fuel. It can only survive by causing us to judge, and create suffering and confusion. The mortal coil needs our dilemma to keep us believing it is all there is, it is all we need. Its voice drowns out the sweet song of the soul. It's very powerful. Just look around you. ironically, death or suicide doesn't shuffle it off for long. we just come back in a new one – unless, like Ophelia, you're initiated into the Sound Current, then you may never need to come back.

The Ghost is Adam

'It's given out, that sleeping in my orchard, a serpent stung me: so the whole ear of Denmark, is by a forged process of my death rankly abus'd: but know thou noble youth, the serpent that did sting thy father's life, now wears his crown.' – Hamlet, Act I, Scene 5.

Shakespeare is taking the oral poison of Iago and upgrading it to the aural poison of Claudius. It's worth reading this verse because it is such a beautiful metaphor of why we were told in Genesis not even to touch the fruit of the tree of the knowledge of good and evil, so damnably toxic it is to man.

> *'Upon my secure hour thy uncle stole,*
> *With juice of cursed hebenon in a vial,*
> *And in the porches of my ears did pour*
> *The leperous distilment; whose effect*
> *Holds such an enmity with blood of man*
> *That swift as quicksilver it courses through*
> *The natural gates and alleys of the body,*
> *And with a sudden vigour doth posset*
> *And curd, like eager droppings into milk,*
> *The thin and wholesome blood: so did it mine;*

And a most instant tetter bark'd about,

Most lazar-like, with vile and loathsome crust,

All my smooth body.

Thus was I, sleeping, by a brother's hand

Of life, of crown, of queen, at once dispatch'd.' — *Hamlet*, Act I, Scene 5.

This is how the ghost describes his curse:

'I am thy father's spirit, doom'd for a certain term to walk the night, and for the day confin'd to fast in fires, till the foul crimes done in my days of nature are burnt and purg'd away.' — *Hamlet*, Act I, Scene 5.

This is how Genesis describes the curse of Adam. Can you sense the same energetic vibration?

'And unto Adam he said, Because thou hast hearkened unto the voice of thy wife, and hast eaten of the tree, of which I commanded thee, saying, Thou shalt not eat of it: cursed is the ground for thy sake; in sorrow shalt thou eat of it all the days of thy life.' — Genesis 3:17.

In our play, through Hamlet, Shakespeare is challenging us to avenge the original, spiritual, mystical murder of our father and rape of our mother. This is the human condition. We are experiencing the effects, but have forgotten the cause. This is the cloud under whose shadow we live our lives. This forgotten cell-level memory is the real, incurable cause of all our ills. Incurable in the mind. The mind does not want a cure. The cause of our ills *is* the mind. The mind is terrified of death because it cannot even begin to comprehend what lies in the undiscovered country.

Shakespeare is giving us the keys and the motivation to reclaim our lost memory, our lost inner kingdom and our forgotten self.

Shakespeare, in drawing us in to a deep empathy of Hamlet's expression of our dilemma, is emphasising how it is now a matter of individual personal choice to stay under the mind's (Satan's) tyranny or to step free. Satan has dominion over our minds, emotions and bodies. He rules us by making us believe all we are is merely the hybrids, his monstrous birth, Cain and Abel.

But now, in this time, the resurrection has taken place in consciousness. It is done. Our soul has overcome 'all the world' and is now free. The way is open. We are all chosen. All of us. Unconditionally. Regardless of belief, race, religion, sexual orientation, or food preferences.

But are we going to choose back? That is the question.

Put yourself in Hamlet's shoes. Would you choose *to be*? To reject ideas of 'normalcy', be seen as mad, come into a pure state of being, of soul, accept what is, seek the highest good of all concerned, find the learning, follow the wisdom of your heart — wherever it may lead? Or would you choose not *to be*? Would you act normal, take counsel from your mind, see only right versus wrong, good versus evil, fight evil with more evil, rail against the outrage, kill or be killed in pursuit of justice and revenge on your terms at any cost, or even kill yourself to escape the inescapable dilemma?

Our focus here is to dig down to the deepest possible layer of Shakespeare's wisdom. Once again the psycho-spiritual level is another fall-of-man-vanquishing-of-Satan-by-resurrected-soul allegory. And even deeper are the keys to what this truly means for us, and how we can follow Hamlet's exampleship.

After the set-up, the plotting splits into two parts.

What it means to choose not *to be*. And what it means to choose *to be*.

Choosing Not to be – Be Hamlet Now

Play with me. Be Hamlet – now. Do your best to experience the characterisations and motivations that drive your own inner conflicts. Let all the ingredients bubble in the cauldron. Imagine it is you who is called to adventure by the spirit of your father in heaven to reclaim the crown rightfully yours stolen by a treacherous, lecherous, murdering uncle. You are. We all are.

'Thus was I, sleeping, by a brother's hand, of life, of crown, and Queen, at once dispatch'd.' – Hamlet, Act I, Scene 5.

Imagine you have an uncle who has murdered your father and also lured your mother into his bed of lies before the body of your father is cold. This is what we are all called to do. We are all kings, queens, princes, and princesses of a far greater kingdom than we can possibly imagine. A kingdom guarded by the fears and lies concocted by the part of us that is not *to be*. Never to know. Feel the outrage. Feel the injustice. Feel the effrontery. Was your mother complicit in this crime? She was tempted. She was deceived. She was lied to. She did not trust the Truth within her. She fell. Your father wants her to be dealt with by divine justice. But this doesn't stop you hating her for what she has done. You're a human. You have human feelings and frailties. You loved her – now you hate her. Hate your mother – oh God how foul is this? What are you to do?

'Let not the royal bed of Denmark be a couch for luxury and damned incest.'

What are you going to do? In the mind, the noble way to avenge the crime is to kill the impostor. But this is base and crude. The ghost was vague. What did he really mean you to do? He's making you take responsibility. It's up to you to decide how to avenge your father and bring reckoning to your mother. Vengeance is not our business to make. We must confront the lie with the truth and let nature take its course.

'But howsoever thou pursuest this act, taint not thy mind: nor let thy soul contrive against thy mother aught; leave her to heaven, and to those thorns that in her bosom lodge, to prick and sting her.'

The horror and the effrontery of being in the presence of this foul incestuous murderer thrusts you into a deep depression. You look to your own soul. Your Ophelia. You see the purity and innocence of the *to be* reflected back to you in the perfect mirror that she is. But your sadness and torment frightens her. She tells her father, Polonius, a wise but pompous fool, a sycophant who wants only to fawn and toady to the bastard king. Because he is totally in his mind, he cannot understand you and thus suspects you must be mad. He spies on you. You play along with his games. You convince him you are mad. And you can tell the truth under the shroud of madness to protect you. In this way you can prick the conscience (if there is one) of the pretender.

Panic. Your Ophelia seems too weak to do what must be done. Too good. Too pure. You must avenge. Truth be damned. You'll prove Claudius' guilt and kill the bastard. Deny your soul. Don't even wait for the cock to crow. Do it now. To hell with this pure innocent creature who reminds you of your true nature. Send her to a nunnery, to stay a virgin lest she spawn a devil like you. And right here you do commit the original sin. You banish your soul in favour of worldly values. You have too much respect upon the world, oh sad one.

As did Lear, you banish your soul, your Coeur de Lear, your Ophelia. Like Malcolm, you confess to the sin of the world. You reject your Ophelia saying:

'I loved you once ... you should not have believed me ... I loved you not ... Get thee to a nunnery. I am myself indifferent honest, but yet I could accuse me of such things, that it were better my mother had not borne me. I am very proud, revengeful, ambitious, with more offences at my beck, than I have thoughts to put them in ... we are arrant knaves all, believe none of us. Go thy ways to a nunnery.'

And here begins what looks like your downward spiral on the helter-skelter to hell. You confront your vixen mother. You kill the rat, the unseen good old man, the spy hiding behind the curtain like the Wizard of Oz.

But soft, you're not really falling, you are doing what Jesus did and simply revealing to the devil the truth of who he is and what his crime was. You make him look into the mirror of a dumbshow – a mime depicting in fine detail the very crimes committed by the tyrant king.

At the story level it looks as if you're dithering all the time. Hamlet is traditionally played as the apotheosis of indecision. But if we look deeper at who he is actually representing, it makes stunning sense. Once again, when Jesus did what he came to do to fulfil the law, he had to go into the darkest corners of the world and shine the light of truth. Hamlet's bizarre behaviour, cutting wit, and clowning antics are surely doing just this? Jesus, blaspheming Jew that he was, told the people and the Pharisees what was what. He didn't pull any punches or flinch from the direst of consequences. Is this how we need to be in order to be authentic, true to ourselves, in our own lives? Or perhaps, because all this has already been done by one braver and more self-aware than we, as long as we do our portion (given where we are and what we have to deal with) the gap between the work needed and the work we can do is filled by grace?

As Hamlet, in going into these dark places you are showing us the world is our prison, and the mind our jailer. When you've finished your shadow work, Shakespeare doesn't just abandon us with a sense of loss and tragedy. Hidden in his verse he tells us the soul is the *get out of jail free card*, and saying The Name the 'open sesame' that opens the doorway.

The World is our Prison: The Mind our Jailer

When Macbeth murdered Banquo, who represented the father to the spiritual line of kings who would eventually bring him down, he hired a pair of assassins to do his dirty work. Loosely speaking they may have represented Annas and Caiaphas the high priests who called for Jesus' death. As far as we can tell, they weren't cast as Jewish. But Shakespeare, unfettered by today's racial sensitivities and political correctness, is upping the stakes. When Claudius needs to silence forever the truth in you he hires two gentlemen with very Jewish-sounding names to do the business: Rosencrantz and Guildenstern. In one of many scenes of cutting banter, he gives us this gem of philosophy. Notice how you also answer your earlier question: *'What dreams may come when we have shuffled off this mortal coil?'* Answer: *'I could … count myself a king of infinite space … '.* The mortal coil is more than just the body, it is the coil of the serpent who wraps itself around the soul, strangles it and utters forked-tongued lies in its place.

HAMLET   *Then is doomsday near. But your news is not true. Let me question more in particular. What have you, my good friends, deserved at the hands of fortune that she sends you to prison hither?*

GUILDENSTERN   *Prison, my lord?*

HAMLET   *Denmark's a prison.*

ROSENCRANTZ   *Then is the world one?*

HAMLET   *A goodly one, in which there are many confines, wards, and dungeons, Denmark being one o' th' worst.*

ROSENCRANTZ   *We think not so, my lord.*

HAMLET   *Why then, 'tis none to you, for there is nothing either good or bad, but thinking makes it so. To me it is a prison.*

ROSENCRANTZ   *Why then, your ambition makes it one. 'Tis too narrow for your mind.*

HAMLET   *O God, I could be bounded in a nutshell and count myself a king of infinite space were it not that I have bad dreams.*

GUILDENSTERN   *Which dreams indeed are ambition, for the very substance of the ambitious is mere the shadow of a dream.*

HAMLET   *A dream itself is but a shadow.*

The Mirror of Truth

'Come, come, and sit you down; you shall not budge; you go not till I set a glass where you may see the inmost part of you.' — Hamlet, Act 3, Scene 4.

To hold up the mirror of truth, you first put on a play for Claudius and Gertrude. This depicts the detail of how your father was murdered by having the poison poured into his ear and how the murderer immediately takes his widow your mother to his bed. Unable to conceal his fear of the truth having been discovered, Claudius must flee the heat of the cauldron — *'give me some light, away!'* You sneer at the cowardly usurper:

'Why, let the stricken deer go weep,

The hart ungallèd play.

For some must watch while some must sleep.

So runs the world away.

For thou dost know, O Damon dear,

This realm dismantled was

Of Jove [God] himself. And now reigns here

A very, very — pajock [peacock].' — Hamlet, Act 3, Scene 2.

Gertrude summons you to her chamber to chide you for having offended your 'father'. You turn this back on her and accuse her of having offended your father — and proceed to fully confront her with the truth.

In fear of her life, Gertrude calls for help. Hiding behind the arras is old Polonius spying on you. He cries out too, and , thinking it is Claudius, you run him through with your sword. You thus kill the father of Ophelia, and set off another downward spiral to experience on our behalf.

Before this scene is ended, you forgive your mother, entreat her to confess and cleanse her guilt, and reminds us once again who Claudius is and what it was he stole — the diamond, the Grail.

'A cutpurse of the empire and the rule, that from a shelf the precious diadem stole, and put in his pocket!' — *Hamlet*, Act 3, Scene 4.

Shakespeare has also had Claudius confirm his Cain archetype with his own words, and in so doing, twins himself with the Macbeths and Pilate — right down to the bloody hands:

'O, my offence is rank, it smells to heaven. It hath the primal eldest curse upon't, a brother's murder ... What if this cursed hand were thicker than itself with brother's blood, is there not rain enough in the sweet heavens to wash it white as snow?' — *Hamlet*, Act 3, Scene 3.

Choosing to be — Hamlet's Resurrection

'They [Rosencrantz and Guildenstern] are not near my conscience; their defeat does by their own insinuation grow.' — *Hamlet*, Act V, Scene 2.

With the death of Rosencrantz and Guildenstern, the tide turns for you and the mystical theological revelation for us gets more challenging, but infinitely more fascinating.

In the play, two events now happen simultaneously. Both heavily laden with subtle yet profound mystical symbolism. Symbolism of the Sound Current, that, as we have said repeatedly is current terminology for what is spoken of biblically as the waters, the Word, the wind from heaven – God's divine instrument of creation, the audible light stream that conducts the soul to and from the heart of God and the physical created world.

It is this symbolism that Shakespeare ultimately dramatises as *The Tempest* and foreshadows throughout his oeuvre with allusions ranging from divine music (*the food of love*) to streams, brooks, storms, winds, lightning, thunder, rain, and seas. Even Shylock was recruited as a spokesman for the Sound Current in his foreshadowing to Antonio, (*'But ships are but boards, sailors but men: there be land-rats and water-rats, water-thieves and land-thieves, I mean pirates, and then there is the peril of waters winds and rocks.*) A foreshadowing that now manifests for you.

Now here's a really counter-cultural, challenging paradigm. You are Hamlet. Ophelia is your soul. From a soul-centred viewing point, once you have been initiated into the Sound Current, the soul's spiritual progression is no longer determined by the activity of the mortal body and the inner psychic levels. This accounts for how your soul, Ophelia, can appear to drown but by letting the verse wash over you, you can see how she is chanting the sacred tones and being conducted home to the kingdom of God on the Sound Current.

You, as a mortal being, are fulfilling your karma here on earth, but your soul, Ophelia, has completed its mission and when you drop the body (as you do) you are already established in the kingdom over which you have the divine right to rule. As Fortinbras says, alluding to the Sound Current conducting you home as a king:

'Bear Hamlet like a soldier to the stage; for he was likely, had he been put on to have prov'd most royally; and for his passage, the soldier's music and the rites of war speak loudly for him.' – *Hamlet*, Act 5, Scene 2.

The Resurrection of the Soul

'And the soldiers platted a crown of thorns, and put it on his head, and they put on him a purple robe' – John 19:2.

While Hamlet is violently tested on his voyage across the waters to England, Ophelia meets her 'death' in the waters of a gently flowing stream. As you read Gertrude's account of how Ophelia met her fate, notice the imagery of Christ's purple robe and how closely it resembles Lorenzo's serenade to Jessica (*'Come, ho and wake Diana with a hymn . . . and draw her home with music.'*).

'There is a willow grows aslant a brook

That shows his hoar leaves in the glassy stream.

There with fantastic garlands did she come

Of crowflowers, nettles, daisies, and long purples,

That liberal shepherds give a grosser name,

But our cold maids do "dead men's fingers" call them.

There, on the pendant boughs her coronet weeds

Clambering to hang, an envious sliver broke,

When down her weedy trophies and herself

Fell in the weeping brook. Her clothes spread wide,

And mermaid-like a while they bore her up,

Which time she chanted snatches of old lauds

As one incapable of her own distress,

Or like a creature native and indued

Unto that element. But long it could not be

Till that her garments, heavy with their drink,

Pulled the poor wretch from her melodious lay

To muddy death.' – Hamlet, Act 4, Scene 7.

Probably the most gloriously cryptic symbology (hard to spot) here that establishes the nature of the soul and links The Soliloquy to the ultimate revelation in *The Tempest* is this passage:

'And mermaid-like a while they bore her up,

Which time she chanted snatches of old lauds

As one incapable of her own distress,

Or like a creature native and indued

Unto that element.'

A mermaid is a creature who is naturally at home in 'the waters'. As is a soul.

Initiates of the Sound Current chant the ancient, sacred, names of God (old lauds) in order to leave the body and travel in the soul through the inner realms of light and sound.

To me that speech is a representation of the soul's death and inner resurrection as represented biblically through the story of Jesus. All the mystical elements are present.

I appreciate how subtle, even unlikely, this may seem if you're not familiar with these concepts, so please suspend disbelief. We're far from finished with this theme. We have a truly jaw-dropping conclusion to come – literally!

Failed Attempt at Killing The Christ

'Alack, I am afraid they have awak'd, and 'tis not done: th' attempt, and not the deed, confounds us.' —
Lady Macbeth.

The really interesting point Shakespeare is emphasising dramatically so often is that of the *attempt* to murder the Christ by the Sanhedrin. They may have killed the physical body, but what matters is the soul. The soul resurrected. It was able to do this because while he was on the planet, Jesus overcame 'all the world'. Again, he fulfilled the law, the law of Moses. And brought forward the New Testament sealed through his blood. Nice words — but what do they mean? Shakespeare seems to be showing us.

Back to your playing Hamlet. This event, your resurrection, symbolised by Ophelia's chanting the names on the waters, the brook of David, occurs at exactly the same time as your escape from the *attempted* murder at the hands of the two false friends: good and evil, the impostors, the traitors, agents of Claudius, given ironic, Jewish-sounding names, Rosencrantz and Guildenstern.

Significantly this event occurs upon the waters (*'And the Spirit of God moved upon the face of the waters'* — Genesis 1:2). On the waters of your voyage to England you once again smell a rat. Again, Claudius' rat. And, as was Shylock, Macbeth, and Scroop too all hoist by their own petards, the two foiled murderers have their own justice visited upon them.

Rosencrantz and Guildenstern [the liars, the traitors, the false selves] are dead — but the soul of Hamlet lives on.

As the result of a tempestuous sea battle, a trial on the Sound Current, where your ship is attacked by pirates you are saved. Saved from your pledge to the dark side of your not *to be*.

192

'O from this time forth, my thoughts be bloody, or be nothing worth.'

Enough of all that angry stuff. You are now resurrected. You rise again and return to the country from whence you were banished. You have overcome the twin false selves' attempt to murder you. You are reborn as your true self. You can now choose the *to be*. You have work to do to bring all these aspects back into balance. At the play level, it looks simply as if you've come home oblivious to the continued threat that awaits you. Claudius is now doubly resolved to finish you off. Are you really that naïve to feel safe back home?

And now, true to form as Satan, Claudius engenders a plot and enrols a traitor, to deprive you of your power, your freedom of choice.

The Duel

'I will work him to an exploit now ripe in my device, under the which he shall not choose but fall.' – Claudius, Act 4, Scene 7.

You outwitted Claudius by dispatching Rosencrantz and Guildenstern. The king, incensed that you have escaped certain death, Iago-like, poisons the ear of Laertes, brother of Ophelia and erstwhile good friend and sporting rival of yours, and enrols him in a foul plan to kill you two more times!

Laertes is easy meat. You have killed his father, jilted his sister and driven her insane (so it would seem). He hates you with vilest bile. Claudius reprises Macbeth while it falls to Laertes to take on the Judas role. I know what you're thinking – I thought you said I was now the resurrected me? I did. You are. But Shakespeare needs a device, a way to make sure all the necessary ingredients are in the cauldron. Like any good writer who follows the mythological story structure, he has carte blanche with the order of play. To engage the audience, it's easy to endow you with more than your fair share of pride and competitive need to win.

Laertes is no dunce with a blade and neither are you. Claudius talks up Laertes' prowess to goad you and devises a friendly dual between you and your old rival. To wind you up and play on your pride he wagers six Barbary horses at odds of twelve to nine if Laertes gets more hits than you. Those Barbary horses of Barabbas have travelled through time and space from Richard II's dungeon at Pomfret, to Hotspur's roan (that he would have be his throne) and possibly even to Richard III's demise.

But here's the rub, this scene is another enactment of a scene from The Soliloquy. In following the urgings of your pride you act out the not *to be* for all of us. You will eat of the fruit of the knowledge of good and evil and surely die. In order to fulfil the prophecy, you also must die at the hands of a beloved friend who betrays you. That is the way to avenge your father. This is the opposite of everything the not *to be* thinks is justice. You have to go through this physical death to fulfil the law. Laertes has rubbed an unction of a mountebank on his sword. You are fighting the mortal foil. A mere scratch will kill you. If Laertes can draw even one jot of blood from you with his sword, you die. Nice twist on the Shylock/Antonio scene. But Claudius is still not satisfied the plan is foolproof.

The Poisoned Chalice

'This even-handed justice commends the ingredients of our poisoned chalice to our own lips.' — *Macbeth*, Act I, Scene 7.

Claudius, as Macbeth, as Iago, as the Cain/Satan archetype, now re-establishes the Cauldron of the Grail motif. To double-double the success of his scheme to kill you, he engenders yet another plot. Listen again to Iago's voice this time spat from Claudius' tongue. (*I ha't — it is engendered, Hell and Night must bring this monstrous birth to the world's light.*) Claudius wants to be doubly-sure his plan will not fail. As with

Iago, you can hear the cogs turning in his scheming brain:

'Let's further think of this, . . . soft, let me see, we'll make a solemn wager on your cunnings,

I ha't:

When in your motion you are hot and dry, as make your bouts more violent to that end, and that he

calls for drink; I'll have prepared him a chalice for the nonce; whereon but sipping, if he by chance escape

your venom'd stuck, our purpose may hold there.' – Hamlet, Act 4, Scene 7.

Thus in another fleeting, ten-second scene, just before the duel commences, he takes the chalice of wine and dunks into it nothing other than a pearl of great price. A precious jewel he has already laced with poison, dripping with the temptation of the ultimate power of that line of kings!

'The King shall drink to Hamlet's better breath, and in the cup an union [pearl] shall he throw, richer than that which four successive Kings in Denmark's Crown have worn.' – Hamlet, Act 5, Scene 2.

Once again we have the motif of the Holy Grail and the last supper. The blood, the wine, the body, and the sop. This time passed *by* the traitor – not *to* him. This is Macbeth's diamond, passed to him by the father to a line of kings, his *'eternal jewel lost to the common enemy of man'*, the poisoned chalice he metaphorically knew he was to raise to his own lips, is now the poisoned chalice that not your lips, dear Hamlet it wets, but your mother's.

During the duel your poor mother, the fallen Eve, drinks from it and kills herself with Claudius' cursèd hand. Like Ophelia's death, Gertrude's death is another ambiguous suicide. It is often played as if she knows 'tis poisoned, knows her husband's unforgiven crime, knows her own culpability – she allowed it to happen. But, strictly speaking, it's not in the text.

Ophelia Buried at 'Golgotha'!

'And he bearing his cross went forth into a place called the place of a skull, which is called in the Hebrew Golgotha.' – John 19:17

In *Macbeth* we saw how Dunsinane Hill was used as a symbol of Calvary Hill to where Jesus bore his cross. This iconic scene is symbolised by the trees of Burnam Wood borne to Dunsinane by the soldiers of Malcolm, the rightful king. In *Hamlet* we once more have probably the most iconic of icons of Shakespeare sizzling with secret significance.

If we had asked Shakespeare to strengthen the mystical allusions suggesting you are the Christ and Ophelia is your soul – this remarkable scene finally nails it.

When you return home resurrected, bursting with forgiveness you pass through a graveyard where a fresh grave is being dug. When I say 'fresh' it's more like recycled. This is a grave that has already been used. In it you find the skull that has become your signature icon. Your logo, as it were. If we want to conjure up thoughts and feelings of you, Hamlet, we pick up a skull and talk to it. It matters less whose skull it was, than whose grave was being prepared.

Ophelia's.

Allow the import of this symbology to sink in. Ophelia's body was being buried in *the place of a skull!*

In Hebrew *place of a skull* translates to Golgotha. In Latin, Calvary!

Ophelia is buried in a grave symbolising the very place Jesus was crucified and the Christ rose. The *place of a skull* – so called because, like Ophelia's grave, it was where the skulls of many a commoner's body lay to rot. And, because the coroner had decreed Ophelia's death to be suicide, much to the chagrin of her brother Laertes, she too was laid in unsanctified ground outside the city walls.

And here's where Shakespeare shakes The Spear of Longinus at Christianity.

Did Jesus Commit Suicide?

It is a moot point whether Ophelia took her own life or not. Gertrude's account makes it look more accidental. Much to the dismay of Laertes, she is grudgingly given a perfunctory, quasi-Christian funeral by the *churlish priest* – outside the city walls, in an unsanctified grave lest, says the priest, '*We should profane the services of the dead, to sing sage requiem, and such rest to her as to peace-parted souls.*'

But it's the profound theological discussion held between the two grave-digging clowns that, given the Christ symbolism, raises the bigger eyebrow. If they are cryptically discussing the crucifixion, where Jesus knew only too well the penalty for violating the law of the Sabbath, claiming to be the messiah, and allowing Judas to 'betray' him – did he commit suicide? Jesus – what a question! Ophelia is having a quasi-Christian burial and even this outrages our first clown. Act Five, Scene One.

FIRST CLOWN

It must be 'se offendendo'; it cannot be else. For here lies the point: if I drown myself wittingly, it argues an act: and an act hath three branches: it is, to act, to do, to perform: argal, she drowned herself wittingly.

SECOND CLOWN

Nay, but hear you, goodman delver, –

FIRST CLOWN

Give me leave. Here lies the water; good: here stands the man; good; if the man go to this water, and drown himself, it is, will he, nill he, he goes, – mark you that; but if the water come to him and drown him, he drowns not himself: argal, he that is not guilty of his own death shortens not his own life.

SECOND CLOWN

But is this law?

FIRST CLOWN

Ay, marry, is't; crowner's quest law.

Crowner's Quest law? This is likely a malapropism of 'Coroner's Inquest Law' A spurious, capricious, self-righteous law that merely offends the living and has no impact on the dead.

I confess I have had this question in my mind a few times. Why would Jesus provoke the fierce guardians of the Law of Moses knowing the mortal outcome? Because this was a key aspect of his ministry. He came to fulfil the law, not destroy it. And part of this was to clarify what was really intended in the scriptures. He did this not only through the deeper essence of his teachings, but also through his example. An example, as Shakespeare was only too well aware, neither the Sanhedrin nor the institutionalised Church understands let alone follows.

There is a huge gulf between the true teachings of Jesus and the dogma of Christianity. The dogma lives in our mind. The Truth in our soul. The Truth is where Shakespeare's words are pointing.

Shakespeare is clearly continuing Jesus' true ministry. To this day, very few people really know what the Christ action fulfilled. We on this planet are still a very primitive tribe of people. Today is only in the year of 2016 CE. What's this as a fraction of, say, 30 billion years, the estimated lifetime of our universe from the first Big Bang to the Second?

Forgiveness of Self

Now, before you die again, ascend to the brightest heaven of invention and vanquish the Serpent that wears your father's crown, you have one more task.

You are going to humble yourself and ask for your 'madness' to take the blame for your delinquency. You apologise, not only to Laertes, but to Claudius! You have truly embodied the attributes of God: grace, mercy, and forgiveness.

N.B., your example is not about forgiving them their trespasses, but in allowing them the inner peace of forgiving you. This is quite a gesture. Now it is Laertes' time to play Judas, feign love of you, and then strike you a fatal blow when your back is turned.

'I do receive your offer'd love like love, and will not wrong it.' — Hamlet, Act 5, Scene 2.

As did Henry V, you give short shrift to liars and traitors. They forfeit divine aid and have their own 'justice' returned to them. Gertrude dies of the poison placed in the chalice by Claudius, you die of the poisoned rapier, Laertes is also pierced by his own blade anointed with his own poison. And you strike Claudius the vanquishing blow letting his own poison kill him. And now your work is done, you die your final death. But not before you charge Horatio, your friend and beloved disciple (John the Beloved) to hold with the pain of your parting so you can tell the world your story (so they will know the truth of their own entrapment).

'Absent thee from Felicity awhile, and in this harsh world draw thy breath in pain, to tell my story.' — Hamlet, Act 5, Scene 2.

All this you had to do. It was written. Only through your death, your blood, could the law be fulfilled so the soul could hear the sound and be free to go home.

Was *Hamlet* really a tragedy? Was the Jesus story a tragedy? Of course not. In *Hamlet* Satan's rule was ended by his own poison. Laertes, Hamlet and Gertrude were all forgiven. The soul of Hamlet, Ophelia, may have dropped the body, but through chanting those sacred tones was drawn home on its enterprise of great pith and moment.

In the Jesus story, if he hadn't died in exactly the way he did, he would not have resurrected and fulfilled the law of Moses. If he hadn't resurrected the soul would still be in prison — until some other anointed soul had come forward to fulfil the law exactly as it had been set up by God in the beginning. The work Jesus did was for the soul of man. That resurrected consciousness is within every living, breathing soul on earth. And whoever chooses to awaken regardless of race, creed, colour of skin, sexual orientation, or personal circumstance has the divine, unstoppable, ordained right to claim their inner kingdom. All we have to do is choose back.

According to Shakespeare's symbolism, choosing back is to choose to be initiated into the Sound Current.

The *To Be* is the Way — the Name is the Key

'I am the way, the truth, and the life: no man cometh unto the Father, but by me.' — John 14:5–7.

Shakespeare was using the same symbols and metaphors as the Bible — but he was dramatising them in ways to liberate the meaning from the pale caste of dogma. Where Jesus would say the 'I am' Shakespeare would say the 'to be'. The *I am* and the *to be* are not the man, but the soul — it refers to all of us, we are all the *I am* and we are all the *to be*. Apparently, Jesus was the champion who liberated the 'soul of man' in all mankind. The way out of the prison of the world was not through the Church, but through the soul. There's no need to believe in Jesus or anyone in order to be saved. We are saved. We now need to save ourselves from the delusion that we are the being the mind tells us we are.

Not that it feels like a need exactly – it's an option. As I understand them, according to the teachings, of which Shakespeare was clearly a master, the key to the soul is the Name, the Name of Action, the sacred Name, the HU and the specific Names of God that emanate from it. These are given to anyone who asks and is willing to do the inner work to prepare the consciousness to receive the initiation, the connection of the soul to the Sound Current and be drawn home with music and melodious lay. There's only one way out of the prison, and 7.4 billion ways to find that way. It takes work, dedication, discipline, devotion, and the willingness to find joy and happiness in the midst of personal tragedy, pain, loss, and disease.

There are no conditions attached – except one. We must have sufficient soul awareness (or whatever we call it) to hear and feel the quiet inner call above the clamour and drama of the mind and the emotions. It makes very little sense, there's no mind-set or paradigm oven-ready in our culture. So from a worldly perspective the glamour of the earthly plane and the psychic levels has a lot more appeal than meagre lead. But look at Bassanio, he gave and hazarded all and found his prize, the divine Portia and Heaven.

The usurper Claudius won't just roll over and let you through his gauntlet. You still have to do the inner work to vanquish him, the Rosencrantz, the Guildenstern, the Iago and the Falstaff.

Were Claudius, Rosencrantz and Guildenstern all forgiven? Was Satan and all his devils and demons?

We'll have to wait till the next facet of our diamond is revealed before our hunger for the ultimate truth is finally sated. I see Prospero's Isle glinting on the horizon. A fierce tempest is brewing. A ship is about to founder on the rocks. A frightened young man cries '*Hell is empty and all the devils are here.*'

CHAPTER SEVEN

The Tempest

THE
TEMPEST.

Actus primus, Scena prima.

A tempestuous noise of Thunder and Lightning heard: Enter a Ship-master, and a Boteswaine.

Master.
Ote-swaine.

Botes. Heere Master: What cheere?
Mast. Good: Speake to th'Mariners: fall

vpon this howling: they are lowder then the weather, or our office: yet againe? What do you heere? Shal we giue ore and drowne,haue you a minde to sinke?
Sebas. A poxe o'your throat,you bawling, blasphemous incharitable Dog.
Botes. Worke you then.
Anth. Hang cur,hang,you whoreson insolent Noyse-

If The Tempest was Shakespeare's *final* play, why was it placed *first* in his First Folio?

Because it wasn't only the title of the play — but also the *title of his entire canon!*

What follows demonstrates this and underlines our premise: if you don't understand *The Tempest*, you don't understand Shakespeare — and if you don't understand Shakespeare, you don't understand yourself.

Absolute Forgiveness of Cain and Abel

Fast forward 15,000,000,000 Years.

'Our revels now are ended: these our actors (As I foretold you) were all spirits, and are melted into air, into thin air, and like the baseless fabric of this vision — the cloud-capp'd Towers, the gorgeous Palaces, the solemn temples, the great Globe itself, yeah, all which it inherit, shall dissolve, and like this insubstantial pageant faded, leave not a rack behind: we are such stuff as dreams are made on; and our little life is rounded by a sleep.' – Prospero, *The Tempest*, Act 4, Scene I.

Hopefully, if you're not already 100% convinced Shakespeare is not 'just' poetry, not 'just' drama', not 'just' entertainment — but profound spiritual teaching, you are at least a lot more open to that possibility. If so, when he implies *it's* all over, you have to ask what '*it*' is he referring to? Just this play? Just his oeuvre? Or just this planetary dispensation? Is it possible our wonderful Shakespeare is foretelling the very end of time itself? Not only that — but is he also telling us about the nature of existence — and what reality really is?

I rather think he is.

Compare Prospero with Fred Alan Wolf in *Taking the Quantum Leap*:

'If we choose to regard everything we see and do within the framework of the new physics, then we can say that, to some extent, reality construction is what we do every instant of our conscious lives. We accomplish this construction by choosing among the many alternatives incessantly offered to our minds ... Our everyday senses are not to be trusted ... there is always a hidden, complementary side to everything ... this hidden side is not actually present ... in the case of a coin that lands heads up, the hidden complementary side is not real until it is revealed. Our actions in the world are always a compromise between two such opposites. The more we determine one side of reality, the less the other side is shown to us.'

The staggering implication of this seems to be that it is we (you, me, and all humanity) who are creating the universe *every instant of our conscious lives*. That without us there is no universe. When the last human goes, the universe ends simply because there is not a man to make it exist. This is how it 'says' this in Genesis — if you read it through wide-open, soul-centred eyes:

'These are the generations of the heavens and of the earth when they were created, in the day that the Lord God made the earth and the heavens, and every plant of the field before it was in the earth, and every herb of the field before it grew: for the Lord God had not caused it to rain upon the earth, and there was not a man to till the ground.' — Genesis 2, 4–5.

Denouement

A denouement is the final resolution of the intricacies of a plot in a drama or novel. This chapter is the denouement of this book and also the denouement of the *spiritual allegorical* level of what seems to be in all Shakespeare's plays – *The Tempest*. This play is, I propose, Shakespeare's equivalent of what's called in the Bible: *The Revelation of Jesus Christ to John*.

In the introduction, I made some pretty bold claims:

That while each of his plays can be performed and enjoyed as individual works with no connection to each other apart from the obvious one of their authorship, all 37 plays are *also* connected to each other through a deeper paradigm by four common themes:

A simple paradigm shift from viewing the characters and stories as about *external* reality – to viewing them as metaphors of *internal* levels of consciousness allows us to enjoy:

- ❧ A multi-faceted, extended saga and allegory of the soul's journey from The Creation to The End-Time;

- ❧ All the main characters seen as characterisations of three polar opposite pairs of the core archetypes of human consciousness: God–Satan, Adam–Eve, Cain–Abel.

- ❧ *The Tempest*, as his final play, and '*the tempests*' in each of his plays, are metaphors of the mystical *Sound Current* of God, the divine instrument of Creation, encrypted throughout scripture in diverse terms including: the Word, the waters, and the wind from heaven.

～ The secret of a blissfully happy life and ultimate liberation from all guilt, karma, and reincarnation is open to all through absolute, unconditional self-forgiveness and initiation into the Sound Current.

Having explored ten plays in some depth from a soul-centred paradigm, developed their spiritual allegorical teachings, and made numerous links between them on a number of levels, all I need to do now is wrap them all up and tie them together in a nice pink ribbon.

A Quick Recap

Introduction – The ontogeny of our three selves in Spiritual Psychology. Mirroring the recapitulation of the phylogeny in Genesis. In English: how Genesis really does make perfect sense when seen as a guide to our psycho-spiritual evolution. The image of God is within us, and so is the universe.

The Merchant of Venice – and Portia's three caskets. The gold, silver and lead choice reveals the pattern of 'three selves' Shakespeare uses in each play. It also dramatises the power of our word, and the essential choice we all now have between law and grace.

King Lear – and his three daughters. If looked at as three inner levels of consciousness, this metaphor confirms Shakespeare's pattern and also his cryptic use of puns, anagrams, and homonyms to communicate profound hidden meaning. As a play it also demonstrates how '*the tempest*' is a powerful agent of transformation and enlightenment.

Richard II – helps us understand the forgotten pain and tragedy of having our true self, the soul, usurped by the twin pretenders 'good and evil'. This accounts for the lingering, incurable pain pervading all humanity as we search in vain for the hidden Truth within.

Othello — confronts us with the cost of not taking responsibility for what enters our consciousness and allowing ourselves to be possessed by a demon. The play dramatises the very moment Satan hatched his plan for the *'monstrous birth'* of Cain–Abel to enfold and extinguish *'the world's light'* of Adam–Eve, the original soul.

Macbeth — is passed the *Holy Grail* but squanders it for *'thirty pieces of silver'* and the material power and glory of Satan. Only when the line of *'Fisher Kings'* is strong enough is the tyrant vanquished and the Grail restored to the people.

Henry V (Including *Henry IV Parts 1 and 2*) — shows how the Spiritual Warrior in us can be awakened. Through clear intention, ruthlessness, and impeccability, we can take the sword of truth, rout the impostors, forgive ourselves and reclaim our rightful kingdom.

Hamlet — personalises the outrage that who we really are (the TO BE) has been deposed by a lying tyrant who rules our lives in our place. Now the soul is resurrected, it's now up to us to do the inner work to vanquish the inner serpent in our own way.

The Tempest — Adam and Eve are reunited in paradise, Cain and Abel are forgiven, and God is finished with this Creation.

Journal work for this section is about changing the judgment habit to a forgiveness habit. The mind has a compulsion to judge. You can't stop it any more than you can stop a dog lifting its leg to pee. But, unlike your dog, you can replace the old with a new habit — acceptance, forgiveness, understanding, and compassion. This starts with observing your judgments as you make them. They can be pretty hilarious. Write your favourites down at the end of each day. See them as how you are really judging yourself — not the other person or situation.

Then use the mantra: I forgive myself for judging myself for …

Keep this up for a month and you will be a happier, more relaxed, more authentic person.

The Tempest: Mirror of The Revelation

'What manner of man is this! for he commandeth even the winds and water, and they obey him?' – Luke 8:25.

*T*he Tempest opens with the sounds of thunder and lightning – an immediate link to the opening chant of the three witches in *Macbeth* and the storm that brought Lear's reckoning. This instantly alerts me to an allusion to the *Sound Current*. Combining the quote above from Luke and the opening speech from Miranda, Prospero's daughter Shakespeare gives us the first clue that Prospero probably represents God himself, and, by pointedly using the biblical symbol *the waters*, confirms the subject is very much the Sound Current, *'If by your art (my dearest father) you have put the wild waters in this roar, allay them.'* – The Tempest, Act I, Scene 2.

In his symbol-heavy Revelation, John refers to the Sound Current in a remarkably similar way:

'And I looked, and, lo, a Lamb stood on the mount Sion, and with him an hundred forty and four thousand, having his Father's name written in their foreheads. And I heard a voice from heaven, as the voice of many waters, and as the voice of a great thunder.' – Revelation 14, 1–2.

At the story level, *The Tempest* has the same familiar theme as all the other plays we've looked at. Prospero is the deposed Duke of Milan who became banished on this Isle after his brother, Anthonio, usurped his kingdom and abandoned him to the mercy of the elements. Prospero is also a sorcerer who uses his staff and books to lend him considerable power to wield over the nature spirits and the misshapen demi-devil Caliban, the monstrous birth issuing from the witch Sycorax and Satan himself.

Foreshadowing the restoration of Paradise by the Christ, Caliban was the rightful owner of the Island before Prospero used his magic to depose and enslave him. Prospero has a daughter, Miranda, who was but three years old when they were marooned 12 years hence – making her a young girl of 15, two years older than Juliet.

Prospero has charged Ariel, an airy Spirit, to summon up the tempest. It is this wind and sound that are the mystical forces that conducts to him a ship containing, his usurping brother Anthonio, Alonso, King of Naples, Sebastian his brother and Ferdinand his son. And assorted others. They are shipwrecked, washed ashore and remain under Prospero's spell. How is he going to exact his pound of flesh? Will he mete out vengeance like Shylock, or will he show mercy like Portia?

Ariel is quick to connect us once more with Revelation, *'the King's son Ferdinand with hair up-staring was the first man that leap'd; cried Hell is empty, and all the devils are here.' – The Tempest*, Act 1, Scene 2.

This early speech looks like an allusion to *'The Harrowing of Hell'* in Revelation 20:12 where it is said between his death and resurrection, Jesus went into all the hells to free the imprisoned souls.

'And I saw the dead, small and great, stand before God; and the books were opened: and another book was opened, which is the book of life: and the dead were judged out of those things which were written in the books, according to their works. And the sea gave up the dead which were in it; and death and hell delivered up the dead which were in them: and they were judged every man according to their works.' – Revelation 20:12.

The reference in this passage to the *book of life* manages somehow to link Mowbray's banished Duke in *Richard II* to Prospero's banished Duke here on this Isle, and the imagery in this opening and throughout strongly suggests the entire play is intended to represent Shakespeare's vision of the Spirit World to which John says he travelled to receive his revelation, *'I was in the Spirit on the Lord's day, and heard behind me a great voice, as of a trumpet.'* – Revelation 1:10.

I'm going to treat this exploration as an allegory of the biblical Revelation and as Shakespeare's own revelation to us as to the fate of his three pairs of archetypes. Are they all represented now we've been washed ashore on Prospero's Isle – and if so, how?

Unsurprisingly, given the three-selves model, the shipwrecked crew and passengers are washed ashore in three archetypical groups. Can you not see the mirror with all the other plays already becoming apparent? The three 'selves' comprise: The *supplanting brother* and his associates to be dealt with by *Ariel*; *Two murderous* clowns who meet and plot crimes with *Caliban*; and the *king's son* Ferdinand drawn by the sounds of music to meet and fall in love with Miranda, Prospero's 15-year-old, *virgin daughter.*

Before they are all reunited and we learn their fates, they all have adventures through which their characters and archetypes are revealed. But far more important, Shakespeare's Intention for all his works is also made clear.

Prospero's Apocalypse

Here's the most extraordinary allusion: John-Roger was a mystical teacher who held the keys to the Sound Current till his death in 2014. He left behind a veritable hoard of thousands of books, films, writings, discourses and seminars. In his 3-volume book, *'Fulfilling your Spiritual Promise'* he says there are 32 Sound Current initiations between the physical realm where we are now and the God realm where we are destined to return. Reproduced here is a *'Chart of the Realms'*, where he reveals the sounds you might hear that let you know what inner level you're working on during spiritual exercises.

If we treat the Henry Quadriliogy as one extended 'play' and likewise the three parts of *Henry VI*, we're left with 32 plays. The exact same number of Sound Current initiations we need to reach ... Prospero's Isle!

According to the Sound Current masters of all the mystical traditions (Including Jesus) the *only* way out of the physical-psychic worlds is through initiation into the Sound Current (or whatever you call it). The *only* way we can hear these high-level mystical sounds is through initiation into the Sound Current. This means *The Tempest* is entirely an allegory of initiation. All the rag-tag characters on Prospero's Isle represent initiated souls who have returned home to the Godhead.

Now here's a remarkable coincidence. Last week, just as I was giving this Manuscript the finishing touches, I received a CD in the post. It was a talk given by John-Roger in Feb, 1972 called 'Initiation Into the Sound Current'. To inspire us to keep up our spiritual exercises, he's describing the sounds he hears on the inner realms of light as laid out in the following table. As he gets to the 'buzzing' sounds of the Etheric realm, he nonchalantly quotes *Julius Caesar*. On the plains of Philippi, just before their final battle, Mark Antony is discoursing with Cassius and Brutus who tease him about the quality of his voice: John-Roger paraphrases saying that Cassius said: *'your voice is so sweet it could rob the Hybla bees of their honey ... the honey of the Hybla bees is the elixir of God where you partake of the life current.'* Then he moves on. Here's the actual quote from the text:

CASSIUS

Antony,

The posture of your blows are yet unknown;

But for your words, they rob the Hybla bees,

And leave them honeyless.

ANTONY

Not stingless too.

BRUTUS

O, yes, and soundless too;

For you have stol'n their buzzing, Antony,

And very wisely threat before you sting. — *Julius Caesar*, Act 5, Scene I.

Quite simply, this is an allusion to the Sound Current on the etheric realm. Honey from the Hybla bees (of Sicily) is supposedly exquisite and also an allusion to the nectar of the gods.

REALM	SOUND
POSITIVE REALMS	
Spirit	Not verbalised
GOD	**HU**
27 Levels	Thousand violins
	Woodwinds
	Angels singing
	Summer breeze
SOUL	**Haunting flute-like music**
NEGATIVE REALMS	
ETHERIC (UNCONSCIOUS)	Buzzing bee
MENTAL (MIND)	Running water or bubbling brook
CAUSAL (EMOTIONS)	Tinkling bells
ASTRAL (IMAGINATION)	Surf, waves
PHYSICAL (CONSCIOUS SELF)	Thunder, heartbeat

Chart of the Realms — John-Roger, *Fulfilling your Spiritual Promise.*

The sounds John-Roger describes as heard on the highest levels above soul, are uncannily similar to the sounds the travellers on Prospero's Isle remark on in wonder: Caliban describes *'a thousand twangling instruments do hum about mine ears'* — John-Roger describes *'a thousand violins, angels singing, haunting flute-like music, and woodwinds'*.

This surely means Shakespeare is telling us that *Prospero's Isle* is a representation of attaining the highest possible level of consciousness available to man while still in a physical body. Also remarkable, in numerological terms, the number of plays, 37, becomes $3 + 7 = 10 = 1$. The number 1 is the number of creation, the primal force from which all other numbers (and thus the universes described by those numbers) spring forth!

So what, we must ask, are these weird characters here for?

'You brother mine, that entertained ambition, expelled remorse, and nature, who, with Sebastian (whose inward pinches therefore are most strong) would have kill'd your King: I do forgive thee, unnatural though Thou art.' — Prospero (to his supplanting brother Anthonio), *The Tempest*, Act 5, Scene 1.

They're there to be forgiven. (More accurately, to model to us the power of self-forgiveness.)

So who are these characters really? Who do they represent? What archetypes do they characterise?

How about the following casting decisions:

- God–Satan to be played by Prospero and Anthonio?

- Adam–Eve by Ferdinand and Miranda?

- Cain–Abel by Caliban and Ariel?

Let us see how this shapes up.

God–Satan: Prospero and Anthonio

The staff of power through which he commands the winds and rains (the very Tempest itself) is clearly that of Prospero. This establishes him as the God (or Christed Jesus) archetype. Anthonio, Prospero's usurping brother, is seen as an incorrigible traitor, murderer, and serial supplanter. Only Prospero's magic through Ariel prevents him assassinating the king Alonso and abetting his brother to supplant his kingdom. As *'the brother who betrayed, deposed and banished the rightful Duke'* it gives great credence to Prospero and Anthonio as the God–Satan polarity.

Anthonio, just like Satan, has no caring, no love, and no conscience. He is a shadow, an empty vessel void of soul. When Sebastian says to him, *'I remember you did supplant your brother Prospero.'* Anthonio, is more interested in his appearance than his attempted murder, *'True: and look how well my garments sit upon me, much feater than before: my brother's servants were my fellows, now they are my men.'* Sebastian challenges him about his conscience *'But for your conscience.'* (Shakespeare wants us to know who Anthonio represents because this is his way of restoring balance and closure to his great saga.) Anthonio replies, *'Ay sir: where lies that? If 'twere a kibe 'twould put me to my slipper: but I feel not this deity in my bosom.'* – The Tempest, Act 2, Scene I.

He is telling us he has no soul to prick him. And immediately segues into a grubby, cowardly plan to murder Alonso, King of Naples in his sleep and have Sebastian, his brother supplant him! He has no other motivation yet evident than betrayal, murder and supplanting.

Prospero, on the other hand, has absolute power over them all and ultimately offers mercy and forgiveness – the attributes of God. *'It is an attribute to God himself: and earthly power doth then show likest God's when mercy seasons justice ... '* – Portia, *The Merchant of Venice*, Act 4, Scene I.

Adam–Eve: Ferdinand and Miranda

Meanwhile Prince Ferdinand, separated from the king's party, has been inextricably drawn to Miranda by the sounds and music of the Isle. As Romeo recognises Juliet as his other self, Bassanio likewise Portia, Ferdinand as Adam instantly falls in love with Miranda, his Eve. He has been led to her by the strange, mystical sounds and music that we now recognise as the Sound Current. That's what the Sound Current does, it takes us home from the world of Satan to the world of God where we belong. Remember this from *The Merchant*: '*Come ho, and wake Diana with a hymn! With sweetest touches pierce your mistress' ear, and draw her home with music.*' – Lorenzo, *The Merchant of Venice*, Act 5, Scene 1.

Ferdinand remarks on the music too often and too specifically for it to be anything other. Although its meaning has been understandably unrecognised for hundreds of years by directors, scholars, and performers alike, these strange sounds are a palpable presence running very purposefully through the play – from thunder and lightning to divine humming.

As Ferdinand echoes Lorenzo with: '*Thence I have followed it, or it hath drawn me rather*': If Prospero personifies God, the Sounds and music are God's voice, the Word, the sounds of the waters whose source we cannot see, only hear. Ferdinand himself tells us the music waits upon some god.

'*Where should this music be? I' th' air, or th'earth? It sounds no more; and sure it waits upon some god o' th' Island. Sitting on a bank, weeping again the King my father's wrack, this music crept by me upon the waters, allaying both their fury and my passion with its sweet air. Thence I have followed it, or it hath drawn me rather. But 'tis gone. No, it begins again.*' – Ferdinand, *The Tempest*, Act I, Scene 2.

With no hesitation, Ferdinand asks to marry Miranda. And she wants him just as urgently. Just as Bassanio had to prove to '*the (absent) father*' he was made of the same metal as the soul, Prospero too makes Ferdinand pass some tests to confirm his archetype.

Unlike many of the women cast as soul, Miranda is not directly referred to as divine. But at a mere 15 years, her character is classically naive and innocent. And there are three good examples that establish her indirectly:

She recognises the divine in Ferdinand – implying he is a mirror of her own divinity: '*I might call him a thing divine, for nothing natural I ever saw so noble.*'

Sometime later, while enduring his test, he returns the compliment with a powerful allusion to the biblical Christ: '*The Mistress which I serve, quickens what's dead, and makes my labours pleasures.*' – *The Tempest*, Act 3, Scene 1.

She is the object of Caliban's lust and his desire to violate her purity. This speaks as much of Caliban as fulfilling Iago's pledge to bring the monstrous birth to the world's light, as it establishes Miranda in the soul role.

Pass the tests Ferdinand does. And marry they do.

Cain–Abel: Caliban and Ariel

Caliban is the other incorrigible menace not unlike Anthonio in seeming to lack human qualities. In being the issue of the union of the witch Sycorax and The Devil (Hell and Night) Caliban is no doubt Shakespeare's personification of '*the monstrous birth*' conjured by Iago (supplanter) who also has a primary motivation to violate 'the world's light'.

'Thou poisonous slave, got by the devil himself upon thy wicked dam; come forth,' commands Prospero. – *The Tempest*, Act I, Scene 2.

Remember Iago crowing when his plan was engendered?

'Hell and Night must bring this monstrous birth to the world's light.' – *Othello*, Act I, Scene 3.

We know Jesus Christ has been called 'the light of the world' so it follows 'the world's light' refers to whoever might symbolise the Christ self; in Othello, Desdemona, and in *The Tempest* who else but the virgin daughter, Miranda?

In Shakespeare's inimitable way he confirms this in a short all-telling exchange of banter between Prospero and Caliban:

'I have us'd thee (Filth as Thou art) with humane care, and lodg'd thee in mine own cell, till thou didst seek to violate the honour of my child,' says Prospero. Then Caliban retorts with, *'Oh ho, oh ho, would't had been done: Thou didst prevent me, I had peopled else this Isle with Calibans.'* – *The Tempest*, Act I, Scene 2.

As the tale begins, Caliban born of hag and devil, has one abiding purpose – to destroy Prospero, couple with Miranda and spawn. Even if he cannot do so himself, he is the agent of her violation. When he meets the two shipwrecked oddballs, Trinculo a jester and Stephano, a drunken butler, he engenders a plan with them to murder Prospero and give Miranda to Stephano to be his 'queen'.

'Ay Lord, she will become thy bed, I warrant, and bring thee forth brave brood.' – *The Tempest*, Act 3, Scene 2.

Caliban slots comfortably into Cain's doublet and hose but what of Ariel cast as Abel? There's possibly one of Shakespeare's 'name games' in evidence with the similarity of the names Ariel and Abel. The shared suffix 'EL' is also the Hebrew word for God.

216

In the backstory, Ariel had been imprisoned inside a tree by Caliban's mother, the witch Sycorax. Is this yet another of Shakespeare's genius metaphors for how the soul was imprisoned by Satan, and the Grail, the sweet harmony in the soul, lost to the ear of man? Now he's free, the tempest and the sounds abound.

Prospero freed him on condition he would serve him until it was time for him to be given back the liberty he so badly wants.

Ariel performs all of his services with great skill and presentation. From showing up as fire (Pentecost?) on the ship to his appearance as a great harpy to the three traitors, Ariel treasures the aesthetic. He tends to speak in beautifully poetic verse, even about the silliest things, without ever seeming foolish. Even as he pulls on Prospero's robes, he sings a beautiful little song. Ariel stands in for all that is authentic, delightful and good in the world.

The name Ariel could also be an allusion to the Archangel Uriel. He is charged with delivering the law to the perpetrators of the spiritual crimes. '*You fools, I and my fellows are ministers of fate. The elements of whom your swords are tempered may as well wound the loud winds or with bemocked-at stabs kill the still-closing waters as diminish one dowl that's in my plume.*' – *The Tempest*, Act 3, Scene 3.

Through Ariel, Prospero confronts his usurping brother and his retinue with all their crimes against him. Dressed as a harpy, in a burst of thunder and lightning, Ariel, brings Prospero's reckoning to the men. '*You are three men of sin, whom Destiny that hath to instrument this lower world, and what is in't, the never-surfeited sea, has caused to belch up you; and on this Island where man doth not inhabit, you 'mongst men, being most unfit to live: I have made you mad.*'

Ariel now twists the knife by threatening eternal perdition and making out Ferdinand, son of the king, is dead. When Ferdinand does appear, this motif allows the necessary 'resurrection' (even if symbolic) to become a key ingredient in their eventual forgiveness: '*Thee of thy son, Alonso, they have bereft, and do pronounce by me lingering perdition, worse than any death can be at once, shall step by step attend you and your ways; whose wraths to guard you from which here, in this most desolate isle, else falls upon your heads — is nothing but hearts' sorrow and a clear life ensuing.*'

Ariel is also charged with bringing the very *tempest* upon the miscreants and also the mystical sounds we recognise as the Sound Current, the Word of God itself. This does not add up to the job description of an Abel. Think back to Antonio, Othello, Bolingbroke — that's the Abel archetype.

Ariel is much closer to a representation of the Holy Spirit than a monstrous birth. He brings the manifestation of God's will for the highest good of all concerned. In terms of the metaphor he also acts out, like the soul of man, Ariel has been imprisoned by the devil and is to be freed by God himself!

Good thought, but Ariel as Abel gets thumbs down for me. More reflection is needed on this one.

The Mystical Sounds of the Realms

There is a fundamental distinction between the vibrations of energy we call 'sounds' that we hear normally through our ears and brain, and the 'sounds' of the Sound Current. The Sound Current is not a physical sound — it is an inner, mystical sound not of this earth plane. Ferdinand, the 'Adam/ male polarity' soul archetype, alludes to this by remarking wondrously,

'*This is no mortal business, nor no sound the earth owes: I hear it now above me.*' — *The Tempest*, Act I, Scene 2.

If I wanted to listen to the Sound Current, I'd need to meditate very deeply, chant the sacred names of God and listen inwardly with profound relaxed, concentration. It requires focus, dedication and regular, daily, discipline. To actually, consciously, hear and recognise one of the inner sounds and feel the blissful *Ananda* that it brings is a priceless blessing. Everyone 'hears' the Sound Current in their own way. It's not really possible to articulate – even Shakespeare has been misunderstood for four hundred years. For me, given the cacophony usually going on in my monkey mind, the sound is more like a silence, a pop I seem to dissolve into. But it's always with me, I cannot, do not want, to even consider living without it. Anyone who practices or teaches this atunement knows this. Shakespeare knows this. So why is he having all these diabolical, rag-tag characters imbued with such blessings? More significantly, why have all his plays had, if not a real raging tempest whistling through them, at least some enchanting verse or allusion to a tempest, wind or waters? And why has his finale featured the tempest not only in its title, in its primary function of drawing people to 'paradise' and confronting them with their Truth, but also in infusing and captivating everyone present with these magical sounds and music?

Why? Because the Sound Current is arguably the most important thing for mankind to know. It is our birthright. Not only is it the ultimate way out of personal dilemmas external conflicts and wars, it is the key to absolute spiritual liberation. No wonder it has been hidden behind an intricate network of cryptic allusions as well as lies, camouflage, and forced silence.

Suppose, just suppose, our sole purpose in life is to discover that who we really are is a spiritual being, a soul, and we are here to use this planet as a launching pad to return home to God ... and suppose, just suppose the way to achieve this – misunderstood for thousands of years – is for us to be initiated into the Sound

Current and simply let the inner mystical sounds draw us home … and suppose, just suppose Shakespeare knows this but cannot say it directly because it is too heretical to be allowed by the authorities … and suppose, just suppose he found a way to imbue us with this knowledge first subliminally and then later as it became safer and safer for the Truth to be told more directly?

To Many, the Importance of The Sound is Simply Normal

I fully understand how weird this may sound to those of us brought up in a Western Judeo-Christian tradition. So as you read this final chapter perhaps be open to allow the poetry, teachings and experiences of ordinary people bring you the gift of acceptance and understanding.

'Upon mine honour, sir, I heard a humming (And that a strange one too) which did awake me.' — Gonzalo, *The Tempest*, Act 2, Scene 1.

'Be not afeared, the Isle is full of noises, sounds, and sweet airs, that give delight and hurt not: sometimes a thousand twangling instruments will hum about mine ears; and sometimes voices, that if I then had wak'd after long sleep, will make me sleep again, and then in dreaming, the clouds methought would open, and show riches ready to drop upon me, that when I wak'd I cried to dream again.' — Caliban (receiving a not inconsiderable inner gift), *The Tempest*, Act 3, Scene 2.

Rumi, the Sufi Master and poet says, '*Thy wind invisible sweeps us through the world.*'

Jesus, speaks of, '*The wind bloweth where it listeth, and Thou hearest the sound thereof, but canst not tell whence it cometh, and whither it goeth: so is every one that is born of the Spirit.*' — John 3:8.

When Sebastian strangely drops in the line, '*His word is more than the miraculous harp*'. It echoes Revelation where John says, '*And I heard the voice of harpers harping with their harps.*'

Even science assures us that in the beginning there was a loud sound, '*The universe, and time itself, had a beginning in the Big Bang, about 15 billion years ago.*' – Stephen Hawking

What's going on? Where are they? What is this place Prospero's Tempest has drawn us to?

Act III helps us along aways. Accompanied by '*solemn and strange music*' fantasmic, mythical, mystical creatures appear bearing gifts of food. '*What harmony is this . . . ? Marvellous sweet music.*' And now even Anthonio is smitten by the energy. He sees what no one would believe,

'*And I'll be sworn 'tis true: travellers ne'er did lie, though fools at home condemn them.*' – *The Tempest*, Act 3, Scene 3.

That's us, guys, when we sneer and heap scorn upon those who have spiritual experiences beyond our comprehension. The Prince of Arrogance says '*I'm always right, I cannot understand this, so you must be deluded!*' What's running through *your* mind as you read this interpretation?

Shakespeare is telling us about another world beyond this physical universe that we all have access to. Through Ferdinand again he hints: '*Let me live here ever, so rare a wonder'd father, and a wise (sic – wife?) – makes this place a paradise.*' – *The Tempest*, Act 4, Scene I.

Absolute Unconditional Forgiveness

To understand the very essence of Shakespeare's Revelation it helps to appreciate his approach to forgiveness.

Today, most psychotherapy, personal and leadership development (whether or not it consciously acknowledges who we are is a divine spark of God) takes clients through a process of forgiveness. To divorce it from religious connotations, it's often called: 'healing of memories', 'closure', 'completion', 'resolution', 'letting go', 'coming present', etc.

The prevailing religious perspective in the West tends to say it is 'God' who has to forgive us, and we need to feel guilty, repent, confess our sins, and believe in Jesus in order for him to be merciful.

While Shakespeare might agree with the list of ingredients, based on his treatment of the characters in *The Tempest* it seems he favours a very different interpretation of what the words actually mean. My take on spiritual forgiveness is that 'God' is who we are, the soul within. According to the gospel, the supreme oversoul 'God' has already given unconditional forgiveness to all mankind at the crucifixion: '*Then said Jesus, Father, forgive them; for they know not what they do.*'

What remains is for us to forgive ourselves for our own 'sins'. Sin really means to cut ourselves off from the inner awareness of God. It is primarily through ignorance we do this. From a place of ignorance, we place our earth-bound, rabbit-level, point of view above that of the God-level, highest possible perspective of the great seagull that can see all things throughout all time. This is called 'judging'. Making others and ourselves 'right or wrong' (good or evil). This is *the big temptation*. Either way judging may make us feel 'righteous' and 'important', and in so doing gives us a fix of the most addictive, toxic, hallucinogenic drug in the universe – and it's still legal.

Knowing through direct, empirical, personal experience that I get clear inside when I acknowledge my sin (judgment of the behaviour – not the behaviour itself) and ask my 'self' to let it go by saying for example, '*I forgive myself for judging myself as a bad person for losing my temper.*'

Karma

K arma is rather like electricity. I don't have to believe in it because I know it's there. I don't try to understand it because nobody does. But my life's a lot better if I work with it. Regardless of science and theology, it works for me to accept the idea that all the injustice, unfairness, inequality, etc. I experience in my life and see all around me is spiritually perfect right now and, if not already balanced, will be perfectly balanced through the agency of a higher power. It relieves me of the exhausting responsibility of doing the impossible – putting the world to rights all by myself. If something lies in my personal area of concern to change, then I know the difference and will take action accordingly. Working with the idea of karma gives me permission to live in the present – free from the guilt of the past and the anxieties of the future.

It means if I decide to forgive I can let go and let God. And when I play the 'forgiveness game' (which I also do) I simply hold on to the pain in that area.

The law of karma is unwittingly defined in the well-known aphorism, 'we reap what we sow'.

'Be not deceived; God is not mocked: for whatsoever a man soweth, that shall he also reap.' – Galatians 6:7.

As we saw in *The Merchant of Venice*, it's impossible to balance our (karmic) debt until we sacrifice the pseudo-honour of vengeance, and surrender to forgiveness and mercy.

'Forgiving ourselves certainly seems to go against the grain of our human conditioning. Even the idea can bring up feelings of unworthiness or scepticism that it could possibly work. Yet if we recognize that we are, indeed, divine beings made in God's image, the idea does not seem too far-fetched, and as we look at life from that higher perspective, the idea of holding on to judgments and seeking revenge or retribution begins to seem the far odder Approach.' – John-Roger, *Forgiveness, The Key to the Kingdom.*

Psychologically, self-forgiveness is the key to well-being, health and abundance. We don't forgive 'them' for 'them', we forgive 'them' for 'us'. Until we forgive (the judgment we've made about) them, the actions they made that we feel hurt by continue to hurt us over and over and over again. Look at the ten o'clock news, look at all Shakespeare's 'revenge' plays, when are we going to learn that revenge makes everything worse, nothing can ever get better through vengeance? As someone once said, '*resentment is the poison I take hoping you will die.*'

Prospero Seasons Justice with Mercy

Is this to be the Lord Prospero's revenge? Lingering Perdition?

How Shakespeare chooses to have Prospero exact his pound of flesh, is exquisite. He seems to give them all hell – but doesn't. From *The Merchant*, we remember how the law is fulfilled, but mercy and grace come in to fill the gap between our 'portion' and what's needed to balance the scales. Prospero shape-shifts into a raging, avenging Beelzebub to deliver just enough justice to the malfeasants as necessary. Ferdinand and Miranda remark on his mood, '*This is strange*', says Ferdinand, '*your father's in some passion that works him strongly*'. '*Never all this day saw I him touch'd with such anger, so distempered,*' says Miranda. Once again we see the God/Christ archetype taking the sin upon himself. Prospero heals himself of his distemper as he forgives his brother and Caliban.

What Many Men Desire

Prospero creates a magical banquet for Antonio and Alonso that vanishes whenever they try to eat. Later, at a masque to celebrate the upcoming marriage of Miranda and Ferdinand, Prospero remembers Caliban's plot and abruptly calls the revels to a halt. He sends Ariel to plague them as well; the spirit does so by first luring them with some fancy clothes, then setting other island spirits upon them in the shape of hunting dogs that chase them around the island.

Finally, Prospero confronts his brother and Alonso, revealing his true identity as the rightful Duke of Milan. He demands that Anthonio restore his throne; he also rebukes Sebastian for plotting against his own brother. To Alonso, in a symbolic 'resurrection' moment, he reveals Ferdinand alive and well, playing chess with Miranda.

Now Prospero's work is done. Now mercy, grace and forgiveness can be extended and God can put an end to ... to ... time ... to ... to ... to the world?

'Though with their high wrongs I am struck to th' quick, yet with my nobler reason, 'gainst my fury do I take part: the rarer action is in virtue, than in vengeance: they, being penitent, the sole drift of my purpose doth extend not a frown further; go, release them Ariel, my charms I'll break, their senses I'll restore, and they shall be themselves.' – The Tempest, Act 5, Scene 1.

And he forgives them. All of them — even Caliban, the monstrous birth. The tell-tale symbol — not one drop of blood, no dead bodies!

What he is doing is an example to us of forgiving our enemies in order to have inner peace and clear passage into the higher realms. The unshakable religious belief in the need for God's forgiveness is one of the greatest obstacles to spiritual fulfilment — but perhaps if we can superimpose the belief that God has forgiven us it allows self-forgiveness to occur. After all, who is God if not the self of man? Portia's grace comes to us even if we have too much hurt to feel sincere but simply have the *willingness* to forgive.

'You brother mine, that entertained ambition, expelled remorse, and nature, who, with Sebastian (whose inward pinches therefore are most strong) would have kill'd your King: I do forgive thee, unnatural though Thou art.'

And in uttering this promise, God, receives all mankind into his heart and completes this dispensation of time, space, and matter.

'But this rough magic I here abjure: and when I have requir'd some heavenly music (which even now I do) to work mine end upon their senses, that this airy charm is for, I'll break my staff, bury it certain fathoms in the earth, and deeper than ever did plummet sound I'll drown my book.'

Prospero's 'staff' here could be that that is known as 'the staff of power', the authority of the mystical travellers (who hold the Office of the Christ) to bring God's light and sound into creation. When this office goes – it's all over.

This is Shakespeare wearing his own mantle of power, knowledge and wisdom to reassure us that *'not one soul will be lost'*. Contrary to accepted dogma, without the condition to believe in any God or representative of God, without the need to adhere to any doctrine of religious practice, every soul will return home at the end of time. Symbolically, even Cain is forgiven for killing Abel. We are all on our way home to 'Naples' – the Kingdom of God – under *'calm seas and favourable winds'*.

Shakespeare's Revelation

Here we are at the end of the book. The last page of blank screen blinks blankly back at me.

As promised, I've kept the best till now.

It was almost a year ago when I was still getting over-excited about the three selves, the three circles, and the anagrams, puns and homonyms Shakespeare uses to tell us his hidden intentions.

You have probably noticed I've been using the Sanskrit term for spiritual bliss, *Ananda*, quite often. This is primarily to honour Shakespeare as bringing forward a universal spiritual teaching unsullied by thousands of years of dogma and misunderstanding. Although using terminology found in our Judaeo-Christian Bible these are merely labels for archetypes common to all high-level teachings – regardless of religion or faith.

There's also another, more intriguing reason why *Ananda* has been ubiquitous. This, you are soon to have revealed.

All the time I was writing this, I was bouncing ideas off my wife, Geri (who, unlike me, has a degree in English Literature). She's always too honest for comfort about my writing. So when I saw her eyes light up at what was unfolding here I cannot tell you how encouraging it was. When I announced proudly that Regan was an anagram of Anger, it was she who immediately spotted that Goneril was also an anagram of Religon (sic).

When it came to the three circles in *The Tempest* I found myself getting stuck again. Geri and I often crack cryptic crosswords together over scrambled eggs. We're a pretty good team. To solve anagrams we rewrite the word in a circle to help see alternative combinations of letters.

Caliban Unmasked

*C*aliban, like *Goneril*, is obviously as made-up a name as it gets. One morning, I wrote the letters of C A L I B A N in a circle to see if it made another word. I easily saw C A I N and thought at once that was it! I reported back to Geri. She gazed at it for a second and said in her matter-of-fact way, *'Yes, and if you take the remaining three letters you get … ABL!'*

C A L I B A N is C A I N – A B L

Eureka! Of course, the monstrous birth referred to by Iago was the first fruits of not just 'Adam and Eve' but Satan as well. The Bible calls this Cain and Abel, Shakespeare now personifies them as Caliban.

THE TEMPEST

"Be not afeared, the Isle is full of noise, sounds, and sweet airs, that give delight and hurt not: sometimes a thousand twangling instruments will hum about mine ears."

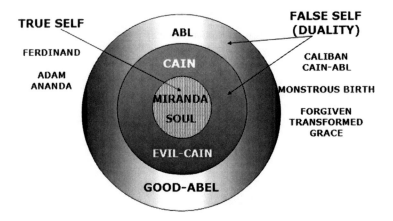

In a stroke, any doubt I had left that Shakespeare really was using these archetypes throughout the plays dissolved into thin air — except for one more wafer thin mint.

If he's coding his intention in anagrams, if Cain and Abel are forgiven at the end-time, what about Adam and Eve? What can we make from the union of Miranda and Ferdinand?

MIRANDAFERDINAND

gives birth to:

ADAM–ANANDA

In Sanskrit, Chid-*Ananda* also happens to be the name of Jesus Christ. And of course *Ananda* is Sanskrit for spiritual bliss. This bliss is what we once knew in the *Garden of Eden* (and can know again in this life — before death) as our home in the fatherhood of God and our brotherhood and sisterhood with all mankind.

Not One Soul Shall Be Lost

There's been a popular myth in our society that unless certain conditions are met, some souls will be damned for eternity to the fires of hell.

Not according to Shakespeare (and the other enlightened masters in his line).

Through his works, he's telling us that even those that seem the vilest, most unrepentant, self-seeking, murderous, pathetic, stupid of us are all just a part of God's expression, and when the expression is over, when the 2nd big bang occurs not one soul will be lost — even yours, even mine.

There really is nothing to fear:

'Our revels now are ended: these our actors (As I foretold you) were all spirits, and are melted into air, into thin air, and like the baseless fabric of this vision — the cloud-capp'd Towers, the gorgeous Palaces, the solemn temples, the great Globe itself, yeah, all which it inherit, shall dissolve, and like this insubstantial pageant faded, leave not a rack behind: we are such stuff as dreams are made on; and our little life is rounded by a sleep.' — Prospero, The Tempest, Act 4, Scene I.

Until then, this final exchange sums up Shakespeare's intention for us to keep on keeping on. As the enmity between Prospero and Caliban (God and Satan) within us transmutes to love, Prospero says:

'He is as disproportion'd in his manners as in his shape, go sirrah, to my Cell, take with you your companions: as you look to have my pardon, trim it handsomely.'

'Ay that I will,' says Caliban, 'and I'll be wise thereafter, and seek for grace.' — The Tempest, Act 5, Scene I.

Epilogue

What I hope I have shown you is how throughout his plays Shakespeare has been offering us one fundamental, existential choice – to be or not to be (who we really are – a soul). In terms of the dozen plays we've just explored, that choice looks something like this:

SHAKESPEARE'S CHOICE

TO BE?	NOT TO BE?
TRUE SELF	FALSE SELVES
GOD	**SATAN**
(DAY)	(NIGHT)
ADAM+EVE	**CAIN-ABEL**
SOUL	MIND
GRACE	RUDE WILL
INNOCENT	GOOD-EVIL
LEAD	SILVER-GOLD
BASSANIO+PORTIA	SHYLOCK-ANTONIO
LEAR+CORDELIA	REGAN-GONERIL
RICHARD II	MOWBRAY-BOLINGBROKE
HENRY V	FALSTAFF-BOLINGBROKE
DESDEMONA	IAGO-OTHELLO
DUNCAN+BANQUO+MACDUFF+MALCOLM	MACBETH-LADY MACBETH
HAMLET+OPHELIA	CLAUDIUS-GERTRUDE
PROSPERO+MIRANDA+FERDINAND	CALIBAN-ANTHONIO
TRUTH	ILLUSION
FORGIVENESS	LAW
FREEDOM	BONDAGE
LIBERATION	KARMA

If it were an easy choice to make, we'd already have made it. But it's a bit like choosing to have a clean face. We washed it yesterday, but today it's grubby again. So we have the same choice again. Every day. Every moment of every day, we have the same choice over and over and over again. Sometimes it even comes down to life or death. When maybe our only choice left is to take or not to take one more breath.

However, without a reference point, there is no choice. Everyone is always making the best choice available to us in the moment. If it we tell ourselves we could have made a better choice – that's a lie. If we want to choose more consciously, more consistently we need the reference point – we need to know who we really are as distinct from who we are not. We need to know how it feels and how we find that elusive pimpernel.

In the soul-centred coaching work I do, I have developed seven questions that I spend as long as it takes exploring with my clients – often assisted by one of my beautiful horses:

- 1   Who are you afraid you are?

- 2   Who do you pretend to be?

- 3   How do you seem to gain from this?

- 4   What does this cost you?

- 5   Who are you really?

- 6   What do you really want?

- 7   How can you be more true to yourself?

In the introduction, I promised to ask you again the questions: who are you and why are you here? I'll leave them with you to contemplate in your own time in your own way.

The Beginning

'And there are also many other things which Jesus did, the which, if they should be written every one, I suppose that even the world itself could not contain the books that should be written. Amen.' – John, 21:25.

This is simply the beginning of a new understanding of Shakespeare, scripture, and ourselves. The first volume. There are twenty-seven further plays to play with. Each so laden with gems, a book like this could easily be written on each. Something about the hidden depths of Shakespeare reminds me of the above quote from the last chapter of John.

Volume II will very much be guided by you. So please be generous with your feedback and creative in your requests.

Meanwhile, you may enjoy this simple spiritual exercise, that I'm sure Shakespeare would have practised.

Chanting HU

'"HU" (pronounced like the man's name, HUGH) is a sacred tone. It is one of the many names for God chanted in many spiritual traditions. This simple chant can quickly bring you into spiritual alignment and give you a sense of peace.

Before you begin, sit quietly for a moment and allow your body to relax. Call in the Light [Holy Spirit] to fill, surround, and protect you for the highest good.

Now begin the HU sound. Take a deep breath and as you exhale, chant HUUUUUUUUU on one continuous note, until all the breath is expelled. Repeat 5 to 10 times, chanting HU each time you exhale.

Then relax for a moment, bringing your attention to the middle of your forehead (sometimes called the third eye), or to the top of your head.' – John-Roger with Paul Kaye, *Momentum: Letting Love Lead.*

If you have questions about this material or would like some support unravelling the mortal coils around your soul, I'm happy to do what I can to help.

I invite you to contact me through my website at www.shakespearesrevelation. com.

I do hope you enjoyed reading *Shakespeare's Revelation* as much as I enjoyed writing it. If you didn't – tell no one.

If you did – tell everyone!

THE BEGINNING

References

King James Bible, God, *c.* 6,000 BCE.

William Shakespeare, *The Complete Works*, Peter Alexander, Collins, London and Glasgow, 1978.

John-Roger, D.S.S., *Forgiveness: The Key to the Kingdom*, Mandeville Press, Los Angeles, California, USA, 1994.

John-Roger, D.S.S., *Spiritual Warrior*, Mandeville Press, Los Angeles, California, USA, 1995.

John-Roger, D.S.S., *Fulfilling your Spiritual Promise*, Mandeville Press, Los Angeles, California, USA, 2006.

John-Roger with Paul Kaye, *Momentum: Letting Love Lead*, Mandeville Press, Los Angeles, California, USA, 2003.

H. Ronald Hulnick, Ph.D. and Mary R. Hulnick, Ph.D., *Loyalty to your Soul*, Hay House, Inc., 2010.

Peter Dawkins, *Wisdom of Shakespeare: The Tempest*, IC Media Productions, 2000.

Norma Lorre Goodrich, *The Holy Grail*, Harper Perennial, New York, USA, 1993.

Michael Baigent, Richard Leigh, Henry Lincoln, *The Holy Blood and the Holy Grail*, Arrow Books, 1996.

Dan Brown, *The Da Vinci Code*, Corgi, 2004.

Eckhart Tolle, *The Power of Now*, Hodder and Stoughton, London, 1999.

Paul Hunting

Since graduating from Bristol University in psychology, Paul has given the past 35 years to pioneering soul-centred coaching and leadership development. He soon discovered a rare talent for using wit, intuition, metaphor, and symbology to enable clients to clear deep unconscious blocks to success. This led him to originate a unique programme of 'Horse-assisted Transformation'.

His first paradigm-busting book, *Why Talk to a Guru? When You Can Whisper to a Horse,* has earned him a world-wide reputation as a facilitator, trainer and thought-leader.

His passion for writing about symbology and practical spirituality guided him through the minefield of misunderstood symbolism to reveal the hidden secrets in the Bible – and then, by serendipity, to this profound work on Shakespeare's plays.

Paul is married with five horses, eight chickens, and a cat. He lives near Stratford-upon-Avon, England.

235

CPSIA information can be obtained
at www.ICGtesting.com
Printed in the USA
LVOW10s0051151216
517339LV00001B/155/P